T0364175

NAVIGATING INTO THE UNKNOWN

The original edition was published in 2015 by Campus Verlag
with the title *Navigieren in Zeiten des Umbruchs. Die Welt neu
denken und gestalten*.

Fredmund Malik

NAVIGATING INTO THE UNKNOWN

A New Way for Management, Governance and Leadership

Translated from German by Jutta Scherer (JS textworks – Munich, Germany)

Campus Verlag
Frankfurt/New York

ISBN 978-3-593-50582-4 Print
ISBN 978-3-593-43423-0 E-Book (PDF)
ISBN 978-3-593-43424-7 E-Book (EPUB)

Cover design: Guido Klütsch, Köln
Design and Typesetting: Publikations Atelier, Dreieich
Printing office and bookbinder: Beltz Bad Langensalza GmbH
Printed in Germany

www.campus.de

CONTENTS

PREFACE

Navigation is the helmsman's art: how to identify our current position, determine our destination, and steer our ship towards it.

The high art of navigation is the ability to get our bearings in unknown territory – that is, when we are faced with uncertain locations, moving targets and a variety of possible routes.

Most organizations today confront such a "New World." This book describes the new methods of navigation required in the New World, including principles of thought and rules of action in conditions of uncertainty and great complexity.

The New World is unknown to us in many respects. So what can we nevertheless know? Perhaps we know much more already than we are aware of.

We know, for instance, that the new will be complex. Managing complexity will be the greatest challenge. This will be true for organizations of every kind: commercial enterprises and hospitals, public authorities and schools, cities and states. We know that all these organizations need to function in conditions of growing complexity; it is also true that this very complexity will enable them to function better and better, and in ever new ways. This book describes the methods and tools to handle complexity, and how systems-cybernetic management helps us master complexity.

As such, we are able to navigate through periods of change despite all the uncertainties we face. With each step we take we will learn more, for that is how complexity-compatible control methods with appropriately designed feedback loops work.

The New World is born from the Great Transformation21, a term I coined in 1997 for the ongoing fundamental change processes across society. It frees us from the organizational and managerial limitations of the Old World, allowing us to function better and to think in new ways and design new things.

It is a principle of mine not to publish any of my books until their content has proven valid in years of cooperation and discussions with hundreds of managers – clients as well as friends – in various top management bodies. I owe my sincerest thanks to all of them. I would also like to thank Jutta Scherer for her insightful translation work, as well as my long-term publisher, Campus Verlag. Specials thanks to my colleague and friend Keith Roberts for reviewing the English manuscript with a critical eye, as well as to Annaliza Tsakona for her comments and to Tamara Bechter, Senior Editor at Malik Institute for her contribution to structure and formulate this book.

Fredmund Malik
St. Gallen, December 2015

Chapter 1

WHY WE MUST REVOLUTIONIZE OUR THINKING

Where am I? What is going on "out there?" How can I find my way? What should I do? How do I even know what my choices are? While smartphones and SatNav have reduced our geographic confusion, in our society of complexity, many of us lack the orientation to fight our way through fragmenting markets, technologies, careers, academic disciplines, regulations, etc. Reliable guidance has become a major challenge for managers of all organizations in society. And everyone else is paralyzed by too many confusing choices and possibilities.

Observations

1. When naysayers abound, telling us what is *not* possible and what *cannot* be done, as is currently the case, this is always an indicator of profound change. What used to be right is suddenly wrong. Many will only see the old in the new, and steer their actions in the wrong direction. In times of change, that is a common pattern.

2. Both business and society face one of history's greatest transformations: from the Old World as we know it to a New World we do not know yet. This transformation will change almost everything: *what* we do, *how* and *why* we do it – and also, *who* we are.

3. The greatest challenge of the New World is its ever-increasing complexity. Complexity is the main reason for the escalating number of local and global crises.

4. Crises originate from outdated organizations incapable of mastering increased complexity. More and more organizations are overstrained, sluggish, inefficient, and paralyzed.

5. This incapacity results from poorly programmed navigation systems, from structures that originated in the previous century, from an outdated understanding of management, and from steering, directing, and shaping with obsolete methods and tools.

6. It is due to this incapacity that more and more organizations respond to the challenge with the wrong strategy. They attempt to reduce complexity so they can cling to their obsolete functions. To them, complexity is something entirely negative. This attitude keeps them from finding effective solutions, and further exacerbates the crisis.

7. The right strategy is to take advantage of complexity. It is the only strategy that creates solutions. Flexibility in responding to complexity is the raw material of intelligence, innovation, and evolution,

for self-regulation and self-organization, and for all major achievements. Complexity and differentiation are the materials from which the New World and its new organizations will be built. The success of the Great Transformation21 largely depends on our ability to profoundly reform the organizational fabric of our society and its management.

8. A sound knowledge of complexity, and the ways of mastering it, is a key resource of a well-functioning organization. Smart use of systems knowledge, feedback loops, and control mechanisms is more productive than redoubling our time and effort. Information on cybernetics will outrank money, and smart delegation to self-organized subunits will outrank power.

9. This is equally true for society as a whole. Its previous political categories, based on the polar opposites of capitalism and socialism, are outdated because in a society of complexity there is not one best way for everything. In their stead, we need a new integration of systems – *human functionism* – as a compass for those navigating through times of proliferating confusion.

Chapter 2

THE GREAT TRANSFORMATION21

"Our very understanding of the world
changes the conditions of the changing world."
Karl Popper

A Sign of Our Times?

More often than ever before I run into people who will explain to me what cannot be done. This happens at all management levels – even the most senior ones – and it includes people who would never have said that in the past.

It almost seems to me as though it is a sign of our times that the number of inveterate naysayers keeps growing. If I count in the waverers and falterers, they are even in the majority. What used to be "anything goes" has turned into "nothing goes."

That said, today's naysayers are different from those of former times. Often they are not "simply against it" – they usually have good reasons. Many are even right, as it is a fact that many things are not or no longer possible.

I take that to be an indicator that the transformation that has been going on in the world, previously at a slower pace, is now entering the phase of acceleration and intensification. People sense that there are fundamental changes in more and more areas of society, and that these changes will be irreversible. But most cannot make head or tail of what is going on. They are increasingly and acutely aware that they lack orientation.

In the Old World, many things *no longer* work because it is coming to an end. In the New World, many things do not work *yet* because they are not fully evolved by trial and testing. That is precisely why it is a key task of management in all organizations to look for ways to make things happen *nevertheless*. It is all about navigating in the turbulent times of a major transformation. We are entering new territory, and we do not know how to deal with it yet.

From the Old World to the New

In all countries around the globe, business and society are going through one of the most fundamental changes that ever occurred in history. We are witnesses to the profound transformation of the Old World as we know it into a New World of the yet unknown. A new order is forming, and so is a new mode of functioning of society – a new kind of social [R]Evolution.

What may look like a financial, economic or debt crisis on the surface can better be understood as something much bigger: the birth pangs of a New World in which everything will be different from the way it used to be. And even if the transformation turns out to be less cataclysmic in retrospect, we would not have committed a strategic mistake by assuming. There is less danger in overestimating a challenge than there is in underestimating it.

A Complete Change

How do you distinguish a genuine transformation from the incremental innovations and changes that always occur in an open economy and a global society?

Part of the answer is to integrate knowledge areas across many disciplines and the relationships between them, as well as accurate knowledge of history. A second part is observation – looking for yourself rather than relying on what the media tell you. A third part is asking questions – not only about the bottom line but also about the top line, turning the world upside down, as it were. And always asking ourselves the same question: *Is this really true?* And a fourth part is systemic thinking: the ability to see and think in holistic terms, refusing to blank out connections, making links, and paying attention to emerging patterns. Plus you need the right methods to bring everything into line.

Or rather, put everything in context – as linear thinking would probably not be helpful. Hans Ulrich, the founder of St. Gallen Systems-Oriented Management Theory, put it in very clear terms: *"Holistic thinking is creative, as it connects things previously thought to be unconnected, thus creating patterns into which we organize individual observations, which enables us to understand what we see."*

The key is to put the pieces together to form a system, a coherent whole. From the integrated perspective, you suddenly notice things you did not see when you considered things separately – they simply were not there. To get this perspective you need models, knowledge organizers, which support the navigation through unknown territory.

The challenge is not to keep looking for new data, as has become the custom – even worse, a brainless mania – in empirical social research. Years ago a different attitude was in order, as data represented a substantial bottleneck. Now we have more data than we usually need, and more than we are able to process in meaningful ways. It is a myth to believe that more data will lead to more knowledge, and more knowledge to deeper insight.

What is much more important is that we question the importance of the data we have. Their significance is based on the interrelationships hidden in the data set or, even more important, the connections that can be established between the factors as they change over time.

Copernicus, who initiated the transformation from the geocentric to the heliocentric world view, did not do so by collecting more data. He had access to the same data, observations, and impressions as all his contemporaries. I believe his particular achievement was that he queried the meaning of these data *in a different way.* This made him realize that the exact same data did not necessarily only imply the geocentric model of the universe, but also its opposite, the heliocentric model.

Navigating in times of transformation requires a similar Copernican capability of the managers of our society. This does not generally take a genius. Most of the time, it is enough to have mastered a certain craft. But which one?

For roughly 1,400 years, hardly anybody had questioned the geocentric view. Copernicus was the man who initiated a major rethink at a time when society was in the midst of a change and traditional concepts were being challenged, sometimes even abandoned. Printing had been invented only about 100 years earlier, giving people easier access to knowledge. It was the time of the Reformation, of religious unrest, and of peasant revolts. The existing social system had begun to totter.

In Copernicus's time, seafaring flourished. Sailors were in urgent need of exact astronomical data in order not to lose their way on the seven seas. The familiar rules of navigation remained in place. The stars, the sun, and the earth with its physical laws were the same as before. What had changed was how their connections were viewed. It took some time for everything to be put together, but when it happened the borders of the known universe had fundamentally been shifted.

This example about the Copernican Revolution is important, as it shows how fundamental transformations can run their course so slowly and spanning such long periods of time that it is not really possible to *see* the shift. You need a trained eye and special tools to observe and even identify great transformations. That is typical of navigation. From the media and the world-wide web we get unlimited amounts of topical news on individual events, data, and facts. But what they imply and the patterns that connect them – that is something we almost always have to find or discover on our own.

When in 1997 I worked on my book on corporate governance, where I sharply criticized the American shareholder approach, I also wrote a chapter titled "The Great Transformation." In it, I analyzed the socio-political and economic change that was underway. Key sources were Karl Polanyi and Peter F. Drucker who, each in his own way, had described such processes before. Both knew each other well. At the time that Polanyi was writing his classic about the Great Transformation, *The Origins of Our Time*, Drucker wrote *The Future of the Industrial Man*. Their mutual influence is quite obvious, though their interpretations differed. In their very own ways, both authors are still relevant today – more so than many newer publications.

The term "transformation" also appears in the title of the introduction to Peter F. Drucker's 1993 book *Post-Capitalist Society*. In it, he outlines the key developments leading from capitalism to the knowledge society and from the nation-state to the transnational mega-state.

By choosing this term, I am integrating some of its previous meanings to describe the generalized concept of a fundamental transformation process for the 21st century. Among other things, this process is characterized by exponentially growing complexity, the emergence of globally interlinked systems, and the dynamics of self-accelerating change. As a result, we are facing historically new challenges. Mastering them will require radically innovative biological forms of organization, cybernetic systems for management, governance and leadership, and hugely more effective social technologies.

In practice, however, working with the managers of business and other organizations, in seminars and workshops, I realized back in the 1990s that holistic thinking was unfamiliar to most of them. Today, sustainability and systems thinking have become boardroom buzzwords.

Understanding this change was important for me in 1997, as I set out to determine the right kind of corporate governance – the kind that we need to make large corporations function reliably. I must emphasize that this applies not only to commercial enterprises but to organizations of any kind, a fact that warrants emphasis as it is often misunderstood. "Functioning" is the most general term I could find to describe the reliable and optimal working of an organization in line with its basic purpose. That was the subject of my book.

It was obvious to me that the then prevailing shareholder value doctrine, which had been introduced with Alfred Rappaport's 1986 book, marked a fatal turn in corporate management. At the time it was still on the upswing. I was convinced that it would not last forever, but that it would cause immense damage on the way until its demise.

In my view, early foreshadowings of a New World included Norbert Wiener's *Cybernetics, or Control and Communication in the Animal and the Machine*, published in 1948, and Stafford Beer's 1959 book *Cybernetics and Management*, which represented a first application of Wiener's *Cybernetics* to the management of large organizations. For me, these works marked the beginning of an exciting journey.

Much of what I described in that book has come true over the years. Yet we probably have no more than a third of the journey behind us – a third of this transformation, which is so much more than a paradigm shift. It is a change in categories.

The Old World of 1997

Let us briefly go back to 1997, the year I published the above-mentioned book. Those born in that year turn 18 this year. They own at least a smartphone and a computer, spend hours on the Internet every day, use a variety of social media, and whenever they need a specific piece of information they google it – a verb that did not exist until recently.

In 1997 there were none of these things. Google was founded a year later, but that was a non-event. Working with algorithms had a history, though, and those who were familiar with it were aware that what was happening was much more than yet another hype. It did not matter that much whether it was Google or another provider. The principle of applying algorithms was a technological reality and available for mass application.

The idea itself had existed since 1948; back then, however, machines had been too slow and transmission lines too weak. That was about to change. The impact would be gigantic, and it would affect our entire life. You did not need a lot of imagination to see that this would involve our options for development in many dimensions, but also our private lives, our civil liberties, and our safety. In 2004, Google went public.

As early as 1975, Stafford Beer, the founder of management cybernetics, wrote about algorithms and the data trail in his book *Platform for Change*. He described how user profiles could be set up and what they could be used for – for instance, to reduce the scattering losses in marketing, which were taking on huge dimensions even then. The techniques described were used for mass espionage during the times of the Cold War. The same book (1975) also had a chapter titled "Science and the Mass Media." Beer anticipated the challenges of the media we are facing today.

In 1997, I wrote about the New Economy hype: "Whatever can be computerized will be – and what can be automated will be." That was a standard topic at my innovation seminars. Digitalization had already set in, but in 1997 there were no smartphones yet.

The first iPhone entered the market in 2007. That alone changed almost everything, and most of it in very radical ways: our communication, many of our ways of living, our interests and values, the questions of data safety and security, all the way to the struggle against terrorism.

As a financial center Switzerland was doing fine in 1997. But only three years later, in March 2000, a financial turmoil would sweep Zurich, as for the first time in over 20 years the stock markets around the globe were close to collapsing. The entire financial system was on the rocks. Then came 9/11, terrorism, America's departure from the civil liberties, the Iraq war, North Africa, and much more. Already in 1999, with NATO's first eastward expansion, a new geopolitical world order emerged that led straight into many of the present conflicts. In 2008, another, even more devastating financial crisis ensued. A financial tsunami swept the world as we knew it, and the supposedly best financial system of all times almost collapsed.

"Classical Management": an Obsolescent Model

It became increasingly clear that traditional concepts of management were about to become obsolete and, even worse, that this outdated type of management was causing unwanted developments. It was simply too weak, and above all too focused on the short term to be able to cope with the new challenges; it was unable to direct, steer or control things in the midst of the new complexity, let alone *shape* things.

That was not surprising, as this kind of management was deeply rooted in the previous century, and thus in a much simpler and slower world. To master the quickly growing complexity, and cope with the dynamics of an increasing global interconnectedness, new ways of thinking and new tools were required.

So, the greatest changes were likely to happen in the fields of organization and management, not in economics. Based on still weak signals it was possible to see that most organizations of society – far beyond the world of business – would face radical change. To cope with these changes, they would need new management systems and new modes of functioning. All management system components, such as strategy, structure, processes, culture, managers' competencies, policies and missions, as well as navigation, decision-making and problem-solving processes and communication systems would have to be adapted and, for the most part, changed radically in many aspects. This development has been ongoing ever since. It is accelerating now, driven by the increasing pace of innovation in almost all relevant fields.

It now became obvious how far-sighted the group around Hans Ulrich, based in St. Gallen, Switzerland, had been back in the early 1970s. It had already begun to move beyond conventional management with a new management model based on systems theory and cybernetics. Linear thinking was replaced by circular-cybernetic models, purely business-administration-focused thinking by holistic, interdisciplinary approaches. In 1972 Ulrich presented his management model (together with Walter Krieg) at the 3rd St. Gallen Management Symposium, which was co-organized by Benedict Hentsch and me – the two young presidents of the ISC's Student Committee.

It was also back then that the first Club of Rome study *Limits to Growth* by Dennis Meadows et al. was first presented. This is over 40 years ago now. Both Hans Ulrich, whose research group I was a part of, and its project manager Walter Krieg were clearly ahead of their time. The St. Gallen Management Model was sensational. It revolutionized the discipline of business administration, in particular in leading St. Gallen University to change its curriculum to focus on management training. This was unique in the German-speaking world. Soon afterwards, systems-oriented professorships were created elsewhere.

Almost Everything Will Change

The great transformation process is far from being over. There is hardly an industry or a sector of society that will not be caught in its currents.

The challenges of change will be even greater for public sector organizations. With their current structures, operations, and decision-making processes they cannot survive. Health and education, public transportation, energy, trade unions, and public administration – they all face fundamental change.

I assume that we have only come about one-third of the way, which means that the transformation is just gaining momentum. In just a few years almost everything will be new and different. *What* we do, *how* we do it, *why* we do it – how we manufacture, transport, finance, and consume, how we educate, learn, do research, and innovate; how we share information, communicate, and cooperate; how we work and live. That will also change *who* we are.

All the social mechanisms that make organizations function will change fundamentally and irreversibly – worldwide. Millions of organizations of every kind and size will have to adapt and be rebuilt, as they no longer meet the new standards. Across all the generations, people will be required to rethink and relearn. This is a unique chance to get rid of the "mental clutter" we have brought from the past decades, and to gain new insight and understanding.

This "once in a hundred years" process of fundamental change is also changing forms of government, the practice of democratic processes, the way in which opinions and preferences are formed, our communication, participation and coordination, as well as the methods used to solve social conflicts and problems.

The great transformation process is transforming the world of business and its organizations down to their capillaries, and it also changes people: their thoughts and actions, their purposes, goals and values, and their meaning in life.

Birth Pangs of a New World

What is currently happening "out there" is much more than an ordinary financial and economic crisis, let alone a crisis of the kind that the world can simply "master" and then return to its previous state. That, however, is precisely what politics and central banks have been trying to accomplish.

Further profound changes, such as in technology and the sciences as well as in people's social value structures – in particular those of the younger generation – in their perspective on and perception of the world, have progressed to a point where they cannot be stopped any more. And we should not even attempt to do that. Instead we should accelerate the change and steer it in a constructive direction wherever possible. Going back is neither possible nor desirable.

Just as a caterpillar, in a quite dramatic metamorphosis, turns into a butterfly for which nothing is the way it used to be, very few things will be the same in the New World.

For instance, the caterpillar is subject to the laws of geodynamics whereas the butterfly has to exist in the world of aerodynamics, which is quite a different thing. To do that, the butterfly needs a very different system of functioning compared to the caterpillar; it needs different sensory capabilities, different neuronal circuits, and a different biological navigation system. And while the laws of geodynamics have not ceased to be valid for the butterfly, their relevance has dramatically changed.

By the same token, the Old World was governed mainly by the laws of money and economics, whereas the New World will be governed by the laws of information, knowledge, insight, complexity, and the dynamics of strongly interconnected systems.

There is no need for forecasts to see that. It is already obvious from various new realities which have started penetrating the structures of global societies ever since the demise of Soviet communism, if not before, and which have been changing the rules of functioning in society at an accelerating pace. The internet is only the most visible example. The collapse of communism was triggered, catalyzed and accelerated by new realities that were beginning to take effect back then. Of course the failure of the economic order played a role, too, but the cybernetic forces of control and communication had a much greater impact.

Knowledge beats money, and information beats power. And this takes us to the core of the New World. Its dominant feature is its proliferating, exponentially growing complexity.

Economics Is Not Enough

Economics-focused thinking, which has prevailed since the outbreak of the financial crisis, does not suffice for us to understand the ongoing transformation. It is much more than a financial or economic phenomenon. It was not without reason that most economists failed to foresee the system breakdown of September 2008, although the first signs had been noticeable in the U.S. stock markets in the summer of 2007, if not earlier. For the general public, the first ruptures in the system started appearing in 2000.

Economic crises, stock market collapses, large-scale bankruptcies, and mass layoffs were all results of naive projections. As always happens, presumed trends were simply extrapolated, and even the most absurd results did not raise any doubts about the methods and ways of thinking applied. Once again, people failed to consider that the economy cannot be captured and steered by mechanistic causal thinking, but has its own intrinsic laws and patterns. The more people talked of knowledge management, the more that very knowledge was ignored. A program for disaster.

With appropriate tools the imminent dangers could be seen much earlier, as mentioned before, some of them as early as in the 1990s, and I made this a standard topic of my seminars, keynote speeches, and publications.

As late as in summer 2008, three months before the Lehman debacle, 98 percent of the U.S. economists as well as the German-speaking economic research institutes predicted, virtually in unison, a 2.5 to 3.5 percent growth for 2008. Apart from very few and rarely publicized exceptions, there was no mention of the storm that had been gathering and was about to break.

Yet, the general blindness for the debacle that was to shake the world only three months later was hardly a failure of the economist community, as is often claimed. It was a sign that something very different was going on, something impossible to detect with the means of conventional economics.

That said, the immediate financial and economic dimensions of the Great Transformation, their significance and risk potential cannot be emphasized enough. They will determine the course of events for many years to come. The most challenging phases of the crisis still lie ahead.

Mind you, with current debt levels there will be no inflation, although that is what virtually all economists believed until December 2014, thinking it impossible that the opposite, deflation, could occur. That was an error. The governmental austerity programs alone, parts of which have been quite drastic, are having a deflationary effect as they strangle economic activity. I believe that the very fact that everyone is sounding the all-clear on deflation is a likely indicator that deflation will continue – and get worse.

What is more, the austerity measures taken are further hindering the ability of many public-sector organizations to function properly. Outdated systems cannot be improved with austerity measures. According to conventional thinking, however, there is no alternative.

A Crisis of Dysfunction

"A city ought to function. To be comfy all I need is myself."
Karl Kraus

Instead of carrying on austerity regimes, new methods and assistance systems enable organizations to function much better for much less money, as many obstacles are removed.

The crisis may appear to be an economic one on the surface, which is how it is still perceived. But it is much easier to understand as a crisis of navigation and, above all, of functioning. This view brings altogether different and far more powerful solutions into focus.

The inevitable revolutions will have the destructive force of a social meltdown, but they also have the potential to generate a new economic miracle and a new, better social order of human functioning. Precisely what course this development will take depends on what solutions the global leadership elites have, which of these solutions they even recognize as such, and which they ultimately choose. The traditional means and tools of politics, society, and business will certainly not suffice for they did much to bring about the new crisis situation once they had passed the peak of their effectiveness.

For the very first time we also have the chance to escape the dichotomy of socialism and capitalism in which so much thinking is caught. We have the chance to integrate the positive features of both systems at a higher logical level, and to develop them into a new, sustainable mode of functioning.

This system will need to have the effectiveness of the market economy as well as giving people the kind of social community they have never stopped searching for in the course of evolution. It is true that even the best proponents of capitalism – like Friedrich von Hayek – maintain that the two systems cannot be combined. But even granting this point, this does not mean there can be no innovative system to integrate these two much-needed elements in a new way, as to this date neither capitalism nor socialism have functioned successfully over a longer term. Systemically, both were programmed for failure from the start.

The ᴿEvolution of Organizations

The main reason for our present crisis is not ideological systems. It is our existing organizations and their malfunctions, which are increasingly becoming apparent. This cause of the crisis has largely been ignored so far. The underlying logic of our current organizations dates far back into the previous century. That is why they are far from able to cope with the new challenges of complexity and dynamics.

This, however, is the moment where they are needed – for it is another commonly disregarded fact that we have long ceased to live in a society of individuals. We live in a society of organizations. Whatever people do, they do not act as individuals but as members or users of organizations. When organizations fail, so do people. Without functioning organizations, people are virtually helpless in today's world.

So, whether the Great Transformation21 can be mastered depends very much on our ability to reform the organizational fabric of society.

A highly developed society has millions of organizations which come in many forms and serve many purposes. In developed societies their number is about five percent of the population, which makes it four million for Germany and 25 million for Europe. These organizations are what form the actual social-structural fabric of a country. Without them, nothing moves.

For eight hours per day, these organizations are people's daily reality and their impact extends far into the nights and weekends. That is where people work, that is where they have to be effective so these organizations can serve their purposes.

These organizations interact, compete, and collaborate; they keep forming constantly changing sub- and super-systems and generate trillions of relationships through their interactions. In a manner of speaking, they are the big black box of society. If the economic and political measures are to be effective, they have to reach and penetrate this organizational fabric.

But how? That is a topic never covered in the countless debates on the crisis – although it is quite obvious that it cannot suffice to focus on just one area or another, such as the banking sector. Rather, we need to find a way to influence the numerous interactions between the organizations of society. It is no surprise, then, that the money spent to help cope with the crisis actually never arrives in the real economy but promptly flows back into the financial system, promoting its self-destruction.

Historically, the epochs of transformation have been characterized by revolutionary machines, such as the steam engine. Technology will be important for the current transformation, too. However, the key to success for the Great Transformation21 will be the ᴿEvolution of organizations and their management.

If we stick to conventional means and methods – as I have pointed out before – a social disaster will be inevitable. On the other hand, if we manage to trigger a major rethink there may even be a new economic miracle – and above all a new social order that facilitates a *functioning coexistence*.

Chapter 3

THE BASIC LAW OF CHANGE

"The pattern which connects …"
Gregory Bateson

Change in itself is nothing unusual. There is always innovation, improvement, and adaptation. Here, we are talking about a very specific kind of change, the kind that will displace the existing to replace it with something new. We are talking about *substitution*.

The Austrian economist Joseph Schumpeter called this kind of change "creative destruction." In doing so, he formulated the basic law of change that also governs evolution in nature.

Schumpeter applies this principle to the entrepreneur. Shaping something, going beyond what exists, innovating – these, according to Schumpeter, are the key tasks of the entrepreneur, as distinct from the "mere" capitalist.

Transformations like these have nothing to do with the kind of social Darwinism which is so rightly criticized. Instead, they help achieve dramatically higher levels of capability. The steam engine – the symbol of the industrial revolution – never did fight the draft animals of its time; it rendered them insignificant.

Horses and cows did not die out because of it. They only lost one of their purposes: they were no longer needed as a means of motive power.

A Map of Growth, Uncertainty, and Creative Destruction

In times of disruption, one of the most important things is to understand what is happening. Knowledge alone is not enough, let alone information and data. Without a profound understanding of what is happening and what it means, it is impossible to act the right way.

This does not mean that we have to understand everything *in detail*. What matters is an understanding of the *underlying patterns* of events. With vast amounts of facts and data, of information and events, it is not that difficult to recognize transformational change, provided you are familiar with the underlying pattern (figure 1).

The paradigm of the Great Transformation is two overlapping S-curves. They are S-shaped because they represent growth processes and there is no such thing as linear growth processes, except in some business schools and economic theories.

In the graph, the red curve represents what I have been calling the Old World. It represents the foundations of our current existence which date back far into the past. The green curve represents the New World and the foundations of tomorrow's world.

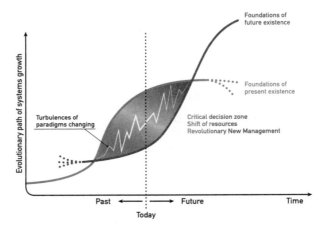

Figure 1: The Paradigm of the Great Transformation21

Between the curves we see an area of increasing turbulences, as the old is replaced by the new. This is the critical decision zone; this is where disruptions take place; this is where the Old World starts dissolving and the New World begins to take shape.

This is the zone where very difficult questions of navigation and management occur. They have never presented themselves before, or at least not this radically. Previous key resources become meaningless; they have to be shifted or newly created.

To find answers, our reflexes cling to the old methods, although they are becoming increasingly useless. These old methods are what have caused the troubles in the first place.

Among other things, one key question is whether people in a "red" business will also be able to contribute to a "green" business, and all of a sudden it is doubtful as to whether you will have uses for even your best people in the future.

This zone of shifts and redeployment is a Black Box: this is what in cybernetics we call a system you cannot look into, and about the working of which you know nothing, while it keeps producing new things you cannot figure out, let alone predict – a zone of disruption.

A zone of uncertainties, but also of hopes and dreams. There is a clash of reason and emotion. There are insoluble conflicts of interest and enormous complexity.

We lack experience with these things, as most people have never witnessed such disruptions before. Previously proven ways of thinking, tools, and methods turn out to be a hindrance rather than a help. Hence, experience can even become a hazard. That alone turns everything upside down.

Navigating into the Unknown

One basic rule of change is: *whatever exists will be replaced*. There are very few exceptions to this rule, including the laws of nature and some basic principles. At some point the red curve representing the old ends and is replaced by the green curve representing the new. Not because the old has become worse, but because the new is better.

Wrong Signals

Once you know the overall picture and look at things in retrospect, you know what the pattern looks like. You also know then what would have been the right decision at any given point – and you might shake your head about the mistakes committed by earlier generations, and feel aghast watching the same mistakes being committed again.

Standing in the here and now (figure 2), however, and without any knowledge about that pattern, you automatically read the wrong signals when using traditional management and navigation instruments, and due to your traditional frame of thinking you will never notice.

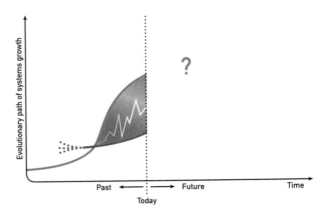

Figure 2: Here and Now: Navigating into the Unknown

In today's world, the signals tell us to continue on the red curve. To the extent that we notice the green curve at all and take it seriously, our old compass warns us not to pursue that route. Only when it is too late do our old systems sound the alarm.

Not One but Three Strategies Needed

"But the ability to create the new
also has to be built into the organization. "
Peter F. Drucker

There is yet another important thing this pattern allows us to recognize. We need a first strategy to take advantage of the red curve as long as possible. We need a second strategy to build the green curve in time to have it when we need it. And we need a third strategy to make the transition from red to green.

It is not only three different strategies that we need, but also three different applications of management and governance. At this point it also becomes very evident where we need real leadership and what it must entail. Leadership is needed for the courage to start into an unknown future, when all visible signs seem to indicate that we should stay in the past.

There are organizations that have mastered change several times in the course of their existence, mainly by making it happen. Examples include Siemens, Bosch, and General Electric, but not Kodak. For instance, nothing could be more useless than having the world's best chemists in the photo industry when the substituting technology is digital. Virtually overnight, Kodak's most valuable asset – the knowledge of its top people – had become worthless.

What is worse, apart from having become "useless" these same people offered the strongest resistance to digitalization.

Substitution and Experiencing Creative Destruction

Substitutions of this kind can be found anywhere, at a small scale and at a large one. From about 1890, the automobile systematically replaced the horse carriage. Similar things happened in the formerly flourishing European textile industry, in the mining and the energy industry, in the steel and the agricultural sector. These are all old examples, but they continue to be instructive.

We have witnessed some of the more recent examples ourselves. From the mid-1990s, traditional telephony was replaced by mobile phones at ever-increasing speed. As mentioned before, Apple put the first iPhone on the market in 2007; at the same time, chemical photography was replaced by digital imaging. For how many of us does the smartphone even replace the digital camera?

In many of these cases – specifically, in the fields of computer technology and photography – I was involved in strategy development myself, and thus was able to see the difficulties managers had in facing up to the new situation.

That was when I also realized what I have been observing ever since: that some managers knew quite well what challenges were lying ahead and what they had to do. They knew the What, but they did not know the How. They lacked the methods and tools to implement and control the necessary degree of change. It is still the same dilemma that managers face today, and to a much greater degree.

Fundamental Transformations

The present transformation from the 20th to the 21st century has its antecedent in the Industrial Revolution. Having begun around the mid-18th century, its key events included the constitution of the United States, the development of the steam engine by James Watt, which signaled the beginning of the age of industrialization, and the French Revolution followed by the Napoleonic Wars. This transformation also led to the creation of the modern university, as well as of the political parties with their ideologies. It fundamentally changed the political structure of Europe, giving rise to a completely new social structure and replacing feudalism with constitutional democracy.

Judging by what has occurred so far, however, the Great Transformation21 is likely to bring much greater and more profound change than previous social transformations. For instance, the university as we know it is not going to survive; also, existing political parties will have to undergo fundamental changes. The ideologies of capitalism and socialism, which have prevailed for over 200 years, will lose much of their present relevance, as they do not provide viable solutions even for our current problems. Democracy, as we know it, is reaching its limits – a fact I have pointed out in my 2007 book on *Corporate Policy and Governance*.

The present transformation is global. An increasing number of systems are more tightly interconnected than ever before, and the pace of change has no precedent. Previous superlatives such as *mega-change* no longer suffice to capture the new dimensions of change.

Another, similarly profound transformation occurred between 1455 and 1517, starting with the invention of printing and molded by the Reformation: the age of Copernicus, whom I have already mentioned at the beginning. Milestones of that transformation process included the Renaissance, the discovery of America, the formation of the sciences, the revival of medical science, music and theatre, and the spreading of Arabic numerals.

Even further back, a transformation of that order occurred in the 13th century, with the beginning of the Gothic period, the birth of the modern city, the foundation of the first universities as centers of intellectual life, and the formation of the guilds as the dominant social structure.

Historically, transformations of this kind have occurred about every 200 to 250 years. They corresponded with extended economic upward or downward cycles, which the Russian economist Nikolaj Kondratieff was the first to explore.

Another common denominator of these periods is that in each case society, and indeed the whole contemporary world, changed so radically within a period of about 50 years that later generations literally had no idea what the world of their parents or grandparents had been like. This includes but is not limited to the social transformations – such as the abolition of slavery, the introduction of compulsory schooling, or women's emancipation.

Fifty years may seem a long time in the life of a human being, even if in historical terms it is a short period. Compared to the life expectancy of someone living in the Middle Ages or the Renaissance age, or even in the times of the French Revolution, 50 years was a lot. The transformations in those times therefore spanned several generations.

Today, 50 years are not such a long period within a person's lifetime. The current transformation is therefore going to be much more profound than those of earlier times: it will be perceived to be more dramatic because the demographic and psychological baseline is different. The pressure for adaptation, which in earlier time spread over several generations, today hits the two or three generations that live concurrently. This demographic aspect is impressive in itself.

To make matters "worse," our present generation is the first in history to have experienced good times only – collectively – which is why we have grown up believing that this is the norm and it will always go on like that. No other generation before has enjoyed a comparable level of affluence, none has been this "spoilt." This is the psychological aspect, and it should not be underestimated.

People of earlier epochs did not expect much of life, society, and the government. They had no illusions. Most were not particularly well off either before and after a transformation, so they had no particular expectations or demands.

Things are different today. In the Western world, the ongoing change is hitting a generation that is better off than any other generation before. As a result, even minor setbacks in the standard of living are perceived to be dramatic. Consequently, the demands placed on leaders, on the navigators through this transformation, are going to be much greater than ever before.

Being Ahead of Change

Just as there is a substitution pattern, there is also a strategic principle that successful companies and organizations adhere to: *Be ahead of change!* They actively make change happen, instead of waiting for it to hit them. They take advantage of the forces of this relentless law of business – and not only business – to start into a new dimension of performance rather than fight it. They keep the initiative and determine the rules. Hence, change is not a must but a want to them. The organization itself determines what happens, instead of drifting along. By outgrowing itself and its previous limits, it in effect substitutes itself. *If we don't do this, others will. It will happen one way or another* – that is their maxim.

Chapter 4

THE DRIVERS OF TRANSFORMATION

> "This way, we find out a lot about details,
> but not about the system as such."
> *Dietrich Dörner*

The Great Transformation is driven by some mutually reinforcing factors that were reasonably obvious as early as 1997. What processes are the strongest change drivers? What is in full swing, what is yet to come? What is misunderstood to be a major trend; what is being ignored?

The answers to these questions would fill another book. From the multitude of factors, I have selected five that, with their mutual interactions, I consider the main drivers of the Great Transformation21: global demographic development; questions of ecology; scientific and technological progress; the economy, specifically pandemic indebtedness; and finally putting all of these together with other factors adds up to a new degree of unprecedented complexity. Managing, mastering, and using complexity is the key challenge.

With obsolete methods and ways of thinking, this is impossible to do. Traditional management has long ceased to meet these requirements; it is only upheld with plenty of improvisation and a great deal of good will. The shortsightedness of it is plain to see. Again, a transition from the red to the green curve is overdue.

Demographics

We are faced with overpopulation and depopulation, with over aging and rejuvenating societies, with a general increase in smartness and stupidity, with growing numbers of poor and of rich people. Caught between these extremes, we will have to deal with unprecedented challenges.

Add to this the disintegration of or damage to social structures in more and more countries, as well as the phenomenon of battalions of young men who see no future for themselves but feel "ready to fight ..."

On Migration and Fortresses of Competence

Low birth rates, aging societies, and the resulting decrease in populations are problems that countries cannot solve with existing resources – but they can do so through immigration. There is no shortage of people willing to migrate – but who will admit whom into their self-dismantling countries, and for what reasons? This is where a term coined by Gunnar Heinsohn comes into play: the "fortress of competence." By that he refers to those countries that are basically open to immigrants – as long as they are superbly qualified. They will not admit anyone that fails to meet their standards.

Other countries, including the European ones, have been more generous, in that they have been accepting lesser-qualified immigrants as compassion weighs heavier than qualifications. The basic problems, however, are as yet unsolved.

The fortresses of competence are headed by Singapore, South Korea, Switzerland, New Zealand, Australia, and Canada. For comparison, Singapore has 9.10 percent students in the top PISA levels; the U.S. has 1.70 percent. With 2.60 percent, Germany is in the upper mid-range.

Inclusionism Versus Exclusionism

There is another important pair of terms: the polar opposites of *inclusionism* and *exclusionism*. In the meaning I am referring to here, it was coined by Robert Prechter, the American Elliott Wave and Socionomics expert. In a nutshell, shortly after the Second World War we experienced a social mood of inclusionism along the lines of "We are all brothers."

Among other things, this laudable attitude led to European integration and its subsequent amendments, global free trade agreements, more openness towards China – and of China towards the rest of the world – and German reunification.

We know from mass psychology, however, that such moods do not last forever. This time, the peak and turn came almost precisely at the time of the millennium celebrations. Ever since then, there has been a notable and increasing mood swing towards exclusionism, according to the motto, "Why care about others? We are busy taking care of ourselves." Current examples of disintegrating social structures and voided social contracts keep appearing in the news.

Several Types of Societies at a Time

Another element of the demographics driver of the Great Transformation is the fact that we live in several "types of society" at the same time. In the past, these would be sequential phases or stages of development.

In retrospect, we could usually distinguish rather clearly between an agrarian society and an industrial one, though there would always be blurred lines so that contemporaries were not entirely clear on what stages they were living in.

Above all, it was easy to go back and forth between the two types, as both had similar shares of manual labor. People were equally qualified to work on a farm or in a factory.

This chronological order has dissolved. Today we live in a society of information, organizations, knowledge, and complexity – all at once. This creates new challenges.

The information society renders time and space irrelevant, which forces and enables us to apply radically new forms of work. I will come back to that later. In a knowledge society, the share of manual labor decreases, as does sensory information, while the degree of abstraction increases. An ever greater share of reality can only be captured by language, not by the senses. The society of organizations loses more and more of its effectiveness, which turns it into a no-results and no-responsibility society.

But there is more. The closed tribal society is also contrasted with the abstract, open, large-scale society and its particular characteristics, such as the disciplining forces of freedom, proprietorship and market coordination, but also its pressure to perform and its freezing coldness. The tribal society, by contrast, met the need for nearness, for security and belonging.

The Society of Complexity Is the Challenge

> "Man becomes mature and able to exist
> as a human being in a complex society."
> *Karl Polanyi*

For my purposes, the most appropriate umbrella term is "society of complexity", and I use it to subsume all other categories described. My subject is management, so complexity and the ways to master it present the greatest challenge of all. I am inclined to consider complexity a sort of development peak, in that we are able to build a kind of management designed for the right objective and the right purpose.

Historically, management theory has largely ignored the subject of complexity, or merely paid lip service to it, which is why all attempts to cope with it have failed. After all, none of all the complex problems, such as the demographic challenges, have even halfway been solved. Indeed they have not even really been tackled, and the same is true for other drivers of the Great Transformation21.

Neither NGOs nor governmental organizations are really aware that management, or something of the sort, is needed in our complex society.

Ecology

We have known since the 1960s that there are environmental problems. A mere 50 years later, only few of them have been solved; others have newly emerged. In St. Gallen we created the concept of the "ecological dimension" of corporate management in the early 1970s. The first Club of Rome report on the *Limits to Growth*, written by Dennis Meadows and a few others, was presented to the general public at the St. Gallen students' symposium in 1972. As mentioned before, it provided an impetus for more ecological awareness. Back then, it helped us include this dimension not only in our thinking but also in our work.

Limits to Growth

There has been much research and dispute ever since. Not everything was strictly scientific; some of the disputes remind me of religious wars. But the Club of Rome's report was one of the early signals that the Old World might be carrying a New World. 50 years later, the dispute has not died down; climate conferences are treading water.

Business Leaders Get Personally Involved

But something else has happened: more and more powerful business leaders take the lead in the ecological movement, publicly and without reservations. They personally commit themselves to sustainability in corporate management.

Fewer and fewer businesses today can be accused of ecological hostility, indifference or exploiting natural resources. When almost every large corporation has its Chief Sustainability Officer, and when the CEOs of some 200 global companies join the World Business Council for Sustainable Development WBCSD (founded by Stephan Schmidheiny) to redesign their companies for the low-carbon economy, it would no longer be justified to speak of a lack of interest, inactivity, or covert depletion.

Caught Between the What and the How

I believe that something else is going on. Some of our top corporate leaders seem to have realized that social and ecological problems cannot be solved with mercy, but only with innovation. Peter F. Drucker has long expressed this view: to solve social distress, you need entrepreneurial solutions and effective management.

We know quite a lot today about what needs to be done. We know the challenges and some of the solutions. The What is quite obvious. For the How, we have no solutions as yet. Again, the key question that particularly the best in management are asking themselves is: how to tackle a matter that complex?

The polarity of the What and the How pervades large parts of society and its challenges. Accusing political and business leaders of being *incapable* or *unwilling* – as the media often do – would be too easy. There may be some that are, but they are a minority.

No, the solution lies somewhere else. Give business and political leaders new, effective tools – and they will be able to solve many of the problems at hand.

CEOs need two things: a new solution for governance and the shareholder approach in their companies, and powerful change management processes. They realize – and say so openly – that today's capitalism needs fundamental reforms and that companies need to focus on a sustainable business rather than short-term gains. That is certainly right. But appeals are not enough. To this date, there have not been any serious, viable alternatives to shareholder governance.

There is a solution, though, and it can be introduced rather quickly. Even Jack Welch, formerly CEO of General Electric and one of the chief shareholder value proponents, has realized that *"shareholder value is the dumbest idea in the world*," so the doors are wide open – wider than ever.

The second requirement is that previous problem-solving approaches be replaced. Small teams, mid-scale meetings, large conferences – all are usually overstrained when faced with such complex challenges.

Even Earth System Governance is put to the test of functioning – at the highest level. A glance at the agenda for this year's G7 summit reveals that, fortunately, this was no longer the sheer business summit it used to be in the 1980s. Instead, it was dominated by the global commons – the topics closest to the heart of the anti-globalization movement. Discussions in El-mau focused on ecological sustainability, poverty, the struggle against epidemics, terror, compliance with social and work standards, and female education. This is yet another example to prove that the What behind the drivers of the Great Transformation21 is moving into focus. How these problems can be tackled methodically is a question yet unanswered.

The minutes of this year's summit and the problem-solving methods used will permit nothing but minimal compromises and declarations of intent, but not solutions.

Science and Technology

What is possible will become a reality. What is considered will be done. That is how I see the development of science and technology, how I have seen it for a long time. It raises ethically challenging questions: you can use fire for both cooking soup and burning down a house, but that has not kept anyone from using fire. It is the same with most technologies that have been useable so far. *We are responsible* for their ethical use.

From Great Breakthroughs to a New Image of the World

Science and technology are among the strongest drivers of the Great Transformation21. I believe that over the next few years we will have a greater surge of new insights in more disciplines than ever, and that we will probably witness the emergence of a new world view.

My work lets me meet a range of scientists from leading research institutes in Germany and the Western world, and my working relationships with Chinese universities and particularly their presidents provide me with insights on their work approaches and their thinking in very different political and cultural circumstances. Yet, I encounter the same situation almost everywhere: people are approaching the limits of their sciences, on the verge of major breakthroughs. And yet once again, the current forms of organizations prove to be major obstacles.

So, a transformation is occurring in the field of science, too. Embedded in the overall social context, this is the source of the strongest and most permanent effects on economic and social development.

Systemic Interconnections Promote Progress

That does not only include information and computer sciences, which have incredible potential in themselves. Breakthroughs can also be expected from materials research, energy research, the life sciences, genetic engineering, brain research, cancer research, and bionics, to name just a few.

Quite interestingly, more and more scientists are stepping outside the "silos" of their particular disciplines. They seek to collaborate with others, as the interaction of individual disciplines can generate highly creative solutions which could not have been envisaged otherwise.

Among other things, I expect that we will leave the philosophy of Cartesianism behind us to advance into system's science in all fields. That would also mean that we will gradually abandon the current curricula and division of academic subjects at the universities, or rather, embed them in another context. In short, creating "the big network" is one of the great challenges in all science.

Irrelevance of Space and Time

Discussions around Industry 4.0 often focus on the Internet of Things, or digitalization in general. Its potential is so enormous we cannot predict future developments, which is why we will have to keep navigating on weak signals for a while.

Whatever can be digitalized will be digitalized. What can be digitalized to what extent is more than most people, perhaps all of us, can imagine. That is not a problem, though. In Newton's time, nobody could have imagined where physics would eventually go.

Digitalization makes us independent of the two great navigators of history: space and time. Exactly where someone was and at what time, used to be immensely important. It has much less significance today. More precisely, it does not matter anymore in terms of *function.*

Structures of time and space are being rethought and redesigned, for instance through part-time models and global collaboration across geographies and time zones. Organizations' geographical coordinates are increasingly blurred and virtualized in the context of cluster organizations, fluid networks, and the Cloud.

Among knowledge workers in particular, both the mode of collaboration and its coordination are no longer defined by the fundamental coordinates of space and time, but by changing work methods. Depending on the individual task, these methods have to be reinvented continually, thus, requiring more self-discipline as well as empathy for others and their work approaches. Free spaces and time slots come and go, as dictated or permitted by complexity and speed.

Managing Knowledge

Technology is the application of knowledge for practical purposes, in particular by the industrial sector but also in the non-business sector: in hospitals, opera houses, the public sector, and the education system – and above all in research institutions, which are constantly gaining importance.

Knowledge is by far the most important resource because it is the key to using other resources (as mentioned before). So, knowledge is both a resource and a product, as its application leads to the creation of new knowledge. In that sense, knowledge is also a means of production.

And while we cannot manage knowledge itself, we can manage knowledge workers and knowledge work. As a result, these two move into the focus of attention, as does their management.

By the time a knowledge worker has completed their training, society has invested quite a lot. It is therefore all the more important to make their work productive and effective. Based on past trials and experiments, I am quite confident that over the next few years we will find ways to measure the productivity of knowledge, just as we have learnt to measure that of manual labor.

But that is not enough. We also need to create the organizational requirements a knowledge worker needs to be productive. They cannot be the same as were needed for manual labor in the factories of older days.

There is much on the news about the "crazy" organizational and working conditions established for Silicon Valley workers. Such organizational environments will become standard for science and technology in many geographies – provided they help create better results.

Scientists and engineers work very differently from other people. In the course of their work they keep entering new terrain, and thus experience new hopes and frustrations every day. Rather than being employees in the usual sense, they are steeped in their research and committed to it heart and soul.

That is why they often find it difficult to deal with superior-subordinate relationships, particularly when their boss is not an expert in their field. They cannot respect someone as a superior when that person does not comprehend what their discipline is all about. Themselves, they often make poor bosses because they are not really interested in managing – sometimes not even in people – but prefer to concentrate on their experiments.

That said, scientists and technology experts need to manage, too, even if this is something they have never been trained for or attuned with.

Economics and Debt

One factor from the field of economics has particular significance for the Great Transformation. It is the greatest debt level in history, which affects all sectors of business and society: nations, states, cities, businesses, public-sector organizations, and private households.

Lehman and the Accelerators of the Crisis

When in September 2008 the collapse of Lehman Brothers Bank in New York triggered what is now referred to as the Lehman crisis, the ultimate disaster was narrowly avoided. The global financial system threatened to be sucked into the abyss. To draw an anatomical comparison, it was like a sudden collapse of the cardiovascular system.

The system has been on life support ever since. There is no theory to explain what has been happening; we are improvising in the absence of navigation. So far, the problems have not been solved. Since Lehman, we have seen the overall debt level increase by another 40 percent, while growth is at best stagnating.

Such an event had been inconceivable to the experts. But others knew that it would happen; only the place, time and occasion could not be predicted as precisely as many would have liked. Related analyses can be found in my books, including a dedicated cybernetic systems model.

Although the vast majority of economists were utterly surprised by these events, afterwards they readily provided explanations and advice on something they had not anticipated.

The Cause: U.S. Companies' Wrongly Programmed Navigation Systems

In my view, the cause of the global over-indebtedness is to be found not in the economy as such, but in the Anglo-Saxon approach to corporate governance and its focus on maximizing short-term profit for the sake of shareholder value. It was invented by *Alfred Rappaport*, an accounting professor. From the accounting perspective this all makes sense – but not from the perspective of entrepreneurially sound, long-term corporate navigation and management.

The shareholder-value-based management of businesses is a prime example of a systematic misprogramming of key navigation systems. It is almost as though the navigators of old had suddenly lost sight of the North Star, and the helmsmen had focused on some fickle planets instead.

Navigation error #1: Starting in the U.S., corporate managers would focus on quarterly reports and stock prices – that is, on short-term shareholder interests. In truth, a decreasing number of these shareholders were long-term owners and more and more of them were professional short-term speculators.

The North Star of right corporate navigation is competitiveness – but its sun is the satisfied customer. When your customers are satisfied because you provide better products and services than your competitors, you generate higher profits and thus keep your shareholders satisfied. This is how to achieve sustainable health for your business. The opposite will inevitably lead to its demise.

Hence course correction #1: Align your navigation with your customers and with competitiveness.

Navigation error #2: The same short-term focus is also the root cause of balance sheet and stock price manipulation (known as "creative accounting"), stock purchases financed with borrowed funds (known as "leveraging"), the bundling of subprime mortgages to trade them on the stock market through real-estate funds (a process known as "securitization"), and the continuous decline of real estate mortgages financed that way. In short, the cause of the ever greater and more widespread indeptedness.

All of these things seemed normal at first, in fact, the sky-rocketing prices for shares, real estate properties, raw materials, and works of art – inflated by credit – were considered the ultimate means of wealth creation for all.

Hence course correction #2: Detach the management of a business from the prices you achieve on the stock market figures. Manage with open time horizons, irrespective of quarterly reports and analyst rankings.

Navigation error #3: People failed to see that the longest stock boom in history was a house of cards built on debt, and that the supposed engine of wealth was actually an engine of asset destruction. What would eventually remain were debts and financial obligations rather than high prices. People failed to see that most of this growth was only financial, not backed by the real economy, and thus largely unproductive.

Hence course correction #3: Tie corporate management to real economic values.

Navigation error #4: In addition to cheap credits and high bonuses for immediate financial gains, money-driven and short-term corporate strategies with a purely financial focus have been the most powerful navigation signals. This policy of navigation via the rear-view mirror led to the greatest misallocation of financial and intellectual resources in history, as well as to the creation of the highest debt mountain of all times.

Hence course correction #4: Reward managers not for the past but for the future.

Navigation error #5: Indebtedness leads to deflation. The flood of money released by the central banks since 2008 in an attempt to fight the crisis has prompted economists almost in unison to claim that the economy is facing dangerous inflation. Their anxious gazes are directed at consumer prices, and instead of seeing signs of deflation they notice reassuringly low inflation rates. The problem is, however, that they are looking at the wrong signal and reading it the wrong way.

Deflation is not a consumer goods phenomenon; it primarily affects assets and industrial goods. Only at a later stage will it be felt in consumer prices. As a consequence, it is harder for us to notice that we already have a deflationary development in raw materials – and that in consumer goods, deflation invariably starts with decreasing raw material costs.

Hence course correction #5: Expand economic theory to form a holistic system.

How to Get Things into a New Order

In a situation like this, even the most well-intended and concerted effort to fight the crisis will remain ineffective if it focuses on the usual economic levers. Even with interest rates at their lowest, everyone will avoid leveraged investments, and consumers will do the only thing that seems sensible: save up their money rather than spending it. All the more so since most people's consumption has reached a saturation level where they can afford to refrain from spending money without risking a shortage of anything essential. People will take precautions for an uncertain future (including one with collapsing asset values and volatile interest rates), for themselves and their families.

Economists will have to accept that most people are not really profit or utility maximizers, indeed are not even economic objects at all, but human beings – usually with characteristics that econometric models cannot capture. Not only conventional business models and management concepts are therefore wrong; in addition, economic management models have largely been incorrectly programmed in many aspects. They must be reprogrammed and embedded in organizations where such mistakes cannot happen again.

Complexity as the Main Driver

The dynamic interconnectedness and interaction of the four drivers described above – demographics, ecology, science and technology, and debt – with their numerous ramifications, generate an immense degree of complexity, which I consider to be the key characteristic of the Great Transformation21.

The challenge of great, increasing and constantly changing complexity is the new touchstone for organization, management, and governance. It is the most significant single new factor in the New World, the greatest challenge for today's organizations and their managers, and the subject of the next chapter.

Chapter 5

COMPLEXITY –
A RAW MATERIAL OF THE
NEW WORLD

"Greater capabilities only arise from greater complexity."
Carsten Bresch

The key challenge of the Great Transformation21 lies in proliferating complexity and finding the right way to deal with it. The management – or lack thereof – of complexity is, as it were, the focal point where all drivers of the transformation meet.

One year before the Lehman crisis, the highly experienced head of a large bank told me after listening to my keynote speech on cybernetic management: "*As long as we keep facing one problem after the other, we will be able to handle it. But if at some point several problems occur at once, that will be too much for us to handle. Our organization is not prepared for that.*" This was a very progressive bank with sophisticated systems. It was robust enough to survive and absorb its losses.

This is one of the typical forms in which the solution to complex problems presents itself to the practitioner. One after the other, neatly separated, with no or just a few interconnections, linear – this is something that Old World organizations are very good at. It was enough for many decades and they have mastered them. This is reflected in the typical organizational structure: almost "water-tight" silos built around tasks that could be dealt with separately because they were integrated and coordinated at the top level. For decades, such forms of organization have been very effective in business, and even more so in the public sector.

The age of complexity, however, requires fundamentally different solutions based on another way of thinking, on new methods and new tools. It requires another kind of information and communication and above all, reliable knowledge about the laws of functioning.

Complexity is the new "raw material", a new kind of asset. For the reliable operation of societal institutions, for a healthy growth in prosperity, and generally for a functioning society, complexity and complexity-compatible control systems will be more important than monetary assets.

Complexity can be ignored, but that will not make it go away. It can sometimes be reduced, for instance through skillful organization. Most importantly, however, complexity can be mastered. It can thus be used to make organizations *more productive, more effective, faster, more flexible, and more intelligent.*

Limits to the Old Ways of Thinking

When there is a lot of complexity, we reach the limits of what the reductionist world view of classical sciences – in particular economics – has been telling us were truths. When reductionist, mechanistic thinking prevails over holistic, systemic thinking, it is one of the main reasons why so many things function less and less as complexity grows. More and more often, organizations suddenly – or gradually – seem paralyzed.

Though we have been tought to consider it indispensable, we more and more often come up against the limits of quantifiability – and yet *we need to act*. We have only insufficient information, and *yet we need to make decisions*. We have no hard facts, so *we need to base our actions on weak, ambiguous signals*.

Anyone coming from the world of predictability, as in business administration or the classical natural sciences, will find it hard to deal with these conditions. Worse still, complexity cannot be seen or felt which is why people often fail to notice it. When things do not work, solutions are sought along the old reductionist paths. But solutions to complex questions cannot be found there – just solutions to simple questions. Implementing these, however, will make matters worse. The result is a vicious circle from which you cannot escape without a good command of complexity.

What Is Complexity? What is Variety?

Complexity is *diversity* – a kind of diversity that can be measured. Its measure is *variety*. Variety is the number of distinguishable states a system can adopt or generate.

Complexity is dynamic diversity that may constantly change. This is one of the most fundamental characteristics of reality. It is the result of increasingly tight networks among people, objects, organizations, and systems which were separate before. Due to their interconnection, the behavior of these systems becomes interdependent, which, in turn, generates even stronger dynamics and self-accelerating change. That creates even more complexity and further increasing dynamics. The result is a self-reinforcing loop.

So, along with the increase in variety brought about by innovation and scientific progress, the main source of complexity is the integration of things that used to be separated and isolated. What happens next? That depends on the elements. In pure mathematics, 1 plus 1 is 2. When I apply math in practice, however, that is not always so. One rabbit plus another rabbit can result in up to 12 more rabbits. So, in this case 1 plus 1 makes 14. The necessary interconnection happens all by itself.

A frequently used standard phrase in management is, "Everything depends on people." That is certainly true, but what is often forgotten is that things also depend on the *relationships* between people.

This becomes quite clear when we look at the exploding number of relationships among elements: it increases according to the formula $n^{(n-1)}$.

Let me give you an example. Between two people there are two relationships. Either can be good or bad. The formula then changes: What used to be $n^{(n-1)}$ now becomes 2 *to the power of* $n^{(n-1)}$. In addition to the number of relationships, we need to consider the number of possible states that each of these relationships can have. 2 to the power of 2 is 4. That, per se, might not be a problem yet – although we hear married couples tell otherwise.

Among 3 people there are 6 relationships, among 4 people there are 12, among 5 people there are 20, among 6 people there are 30.

Six people: that is a typical team size that usually works reasonably well. So, the team structure is able to handle 30 relationships.

Why is it, then, that larger teams quickly become unwieldy? At a headcount of 10, we would hesitate to speak of a team at all, as this is a point where the flexibility and performance of a smaller group will usually tip and the whole thing will begin to turn into a sticky, crippling structure. Is this because of the additional team members or the team manager? But it did work before, right? Now there are 10 people instead of 6 – that makes 67 percent more. Up to this point the line of thinking has been correct, but what has been overlooked is the group as a system. It results not from the number of people but from the interconnections between them.

With 6 people we have 30 relationships, as mentioned. With 10 people, however, we have 100 relationships – 67 percent more individual elements but 233 percent more relationships. And if we count in the number of states these relationships can have, it is 2 to the power of 100.

Inconceivable yet Manageable

It is not without reason that "complexity" is one of the most frequently used terms. There is hardly a presentation or management-level discussion without a reference to complexity – of markets, of products, and/or of processes. In most cases, however, it is only briefly mentioned. There is little knowledge of complexity, let alone practical knowledge of how to deal with it and use it for a better functioning of organizations.

Most people have a rather intuitive understanding of complexity. They do not really distinguish between complexity and complicatedness. They associate it with something difficult, incomprehensible, opaque, and they are basically right. An intuitive understanding like this may suffice for everyday life.

In a management context, however, in particular for senior-level management tasks, a deeper knowledge of complexity is increasingly becoming indispensable. That is true of all kinds of organizations, in particular in the context of the drivers of the Great

Transformation21. Soon, knowledge of complexity will be just as important to organizations as knowledge of people or money.

The concept of complexity is adopted from cybernetics, where it is one of the core concepts, along with control and information, communication, and feedback. That is why cybernetics is one of the most important sciences for management. To this date, however, it has largely been disregarded in mainstream management theory and practice, which is one of the key reasons why more and more organizations have developed more and more red tape instead of ways to function better.

Knowledge about complexity is important when you wish to prevent systems from getting out of control. It is even more important if you want to make deliberate use of complexity – as a source of intelligence, speed, effectiveness, innovation, creativity, adaptiveness, and some more desirable or necessary system characteristics.

All are indispensable for managing the Great Transformation21. To me, management for the New World is mastery and deliberate use of complexity. To do that, we need to understand the laws of nature that govern the phenomenon of complexity. They are just as necessary here as the natural laws of matter and energy are for the natural sciences and technology.

Simple and Complex Systems

Simple systems do not pose much of a problem in terms of control, regulation, and steering. Serious problems emerge – and do so with a vengeance – when a system is complex.

What is it that must be brought under control? Actually, it is not "the system," as we say for short. Strictly speaking, it is the system's complexity. The core questions of cybernetics, then, are these: *How do you control and regulate a system that is complex? What must the structure or architecture of a system be like to allow its complexity to be controlled? What can you do when a system is "out of control?"*

Here, it is helpful if experts in an organization know the *Law of Requisite Variety*, which says that "only variety can control variety," i.e. the control system must have at least as many possible states as the system to be controlled. Named after its discoverer, the English neuro-cybernetics pioneer Ross W. Ashby, it is also referred to as "Ashby's Law of Requisite Variety." It is as significant for managing complex systems as Newton's law of gravitation is for physics and engineering.

This is one part of what makes cybernetics so interesting, and complexity so important. The other is the insight that there are certain capabilities that *simple* systems *cannot* have. As the physicist, biologist, and geneticist Carsten Bresch so aptly put it: "Greater capabilities only arise from greater complexity."

This fact is often overlooked. Numerous books on the subject contain passages whose gist is that the complexity of a system must be reduced in order to control it. That is only half the truth. What is often left unmentioned is the associated risk of destroying the system itself, along with its most important characteristics and capabilities.

In order for an organism to be capable of learning in a higher and sophisticated sense, it needs a minimum of complexity. Below a certain level, learning is impossible. That is why organisms on the different rungs of the evolution ladder have very different learning capabilities, and insects much less than apes. The same is true of perception, of communication, and of the capabilities of thinking and awareness.

The same principle also applies to technical fields: higher performance – for instance, in neurosurgery or avionics – requires adequate complexity of the respective systems.

What do you call something comprising some 15 kg of carbon, 4 kg nitrogen, 1 kg calcium, ½ kg phosphorus and sulphur, about 200 g of salt, 150 g potash and chlorine, and about 15 other materials, as well as a lot of water?

This is a question I have often asked not only my students but many seasoned managers. Usually there is silence at first. After a while, someone will say, "*It's a person.*" Well, quite obviously what I have listed is a series of raw materials. It is what remains of a person once chemistry has done its job … It is what remains when a human being is broken down into its material components – that is, when we take away what makes a living being.

The example shows that it is not the materials that matter. It is the way they are organized, the *order* they are in, the *interconnection* needed to create life; the *putting them into a form*, or *the provision of information* that brings the materials into a *dynamic order*.

What we call reality, and especially life, is not simply matter and energy. It is organized and informed matter and energy.

Conditioned by conventional scientific thinking and an education based on its logic, we fail to realize that it all depends on how these materials are organized. That, however, is the nub of the matter.

That is what makes cybernetics so important. One of its most significant insights is that matter and energy are relatively insignificant for the nature and capabilities of a system. What a system consists of is less important than how its elements are dynamically interconnected. The key factor is the information that *sorts* and *organizes* the basic elements. This is what turns the basic elements into a system.

Complicated or complex?

Complexity has two sides: It represents both a danger and an opportunity. If it cannot be handled it will cause increasing overstrain and the eventual collapse of systems under stress. One would be justified in demanding that it be reduced.

On the other hand, complexity can be the raw material for information, intelligence, and creativity. This is what makes management both difficult but, if handled correctly, it is also what makes it successful.

Complex systems are also known as Black Boxes, because their behavior is inscrutable and incomprehensible. They are unpredictable. It is impossible to say what will happen next. The only option is to wait for their next action and hope you can somehow respond the right way. The greater one's own repertoire of actions, the greater the chances to deal with the situation effectively. Playing chess against a skilled opponent is one example. In some regions, the weather can also be a Black Box, as can negotiations in politics or business.

If something appears highly complex and thus creates difficulties, an immediate reflex is, as mentioned before, to reduce complexity. Often, however, the problem is not complexity but *complicatedness*, which is quite a different thing. For instance, while watches are quite complicated they are the opposite of complex, as they do exactly what they are expected to do. Often we also commit the error to apply complicated solutions to complex systems. For instance, traffic light systems for complex crossings can be enormously complicated. The same intersection, however, can effectively be regulated with a roundabout. Traffic complexity remains the same, but the solution is simple, even elegant – and it comes at low cost.

Most of the organizations we have today are ill-equipped for the challenges of complexity. This is not very surprising, as I have said before, considering that their structures and the way they function date back to the last century.

And while technical departments today have very good control and regulation engineers, it hardly ever crosses anyone's mind that this expertise is identical to cybernetics – and its application does not necessarily have to be limited to engineering tasks. By largely ignoring the ongoing complexification process, many organizations have failed to take precautions and to identify the appropriate regulation and management systems to cope with the present conditions. A systematic application of their control-engineering skills to their own organization could propel these companies into the practice of system-cybernetic managements.

When great complexity is countered only with complicated solutions, we quickly get irritated. One example is the complexity of bureaucracy and the complicatedness of red tape. Kafkaesque bureaucracy – the unworldly kind that takes on absurd proportions and a life of its own – is something nobody wants to experience. When the rule of administrative bureaucracy gets out of control, when regulations matter more than people and people become objects, the amount of red tape drives us insane. On the other hand, professionalism in administrative matters can set an example of effectiveness and efficiency.

Chapter 6

SYSTEMS OUT OF CONTROL?

> "… control and communication
> in the animal and the machine"
> *Norbert Wiener*

"Out of Control!", screamed the front-page headlines when the crisis erupted in 2008, and when just a few hours later the media were full of shocking news reports about falling stock prices and collapsing banks. From New York the financial hurricane swept the world. It triggered a first premonition of what monstrosity had been brought to life in the shape of the present financial system.

Shortly afterwards there was a second "out of control" incident, when it became apparent that people in the global financial centers were basically clueless in coping with the disaster. Collapsing computer and telephone lines, no connections, all lines jammed, busy signals – or no signal at all – everywhere, no way to transmit information and implement decisions, exhausted traders, managers, general bankers and government officials … a system out of control.

The whole thing was referred to as a financial crisis. Well, it was, but more than that it was a crisis of the control systems used in the finance sector. Not only did the blood circulation collapse, but the nervous system, too.

It was by a hair's breadth that a global catastrophe could be avoided. The aftermath is still felt – with stabilization measures in astronomical heights and the largest-scale monetary experiments of all times. The world is deeper in debt than ever.

But no matter whether it is Lehman, Fukushima, the 2004 tsunami, earthquakes in Haiti or Nepal – at some point there is silence and the media turn away, as people get tired of hearing about disasters. At some point, there is a new kind of normalcy – if only the normalcy of a desert where there used to be fertile soil.

Our current list of out-of-control systems is long, and they are clearly visible in drivers of the Great Transformation: the switch to renewable energy has gotten bogged down; an estimated 60 million people – more than ever before – are fleeing from their countries; and there is much more.

Fortunately, there are positive examples, too: excellent rescue services at emergency landings, large fires or mass collisions on highways, disciplined and coordinated approaches, professional collaboration of rescue teams, reliable communication. "Everything under control." That means it works. When something works well, however, when it functions well, nobody notices. People do not pay attention to it, precisely because it functions, so they fail to draw a lesson.

It is when things do *not* function that they will draw attention. The media will report on it, we will take a closer look. The airport in Frankfurt, Germany, had approximately 60 million passengers in 2014 who experienced no problems with their flights. The Beijing Subway transports 9.3 million people safely every day. Neither do the media report on it nor are we interested in reading or hearing about it.

If we were to draw up a list of everything that works well today – it would actually be longer than that of things that do not function properly.

If something is "out of control" this means that its control systems no longer suffice to master its complexity. If it is "in control" it means that the control systems function properly, and so does the overall system. Both go back to Ashby's Law of Requisite Variety (or complexity).

Most of us have experienced out-of-control situations before, for instance when we drive in winter weather and our car starts skidding, or when we go too fast. We have experienced what that feels like: fear, a pounding heartbeat, sweat, panic. And we are familiar with the opposite, the feeling of having "a handle" on things: coolness, confidence, even pleasure – everything in control, mastering the situation.

In modern cars, sophisticated driver assistance systems even take control before the vehicle starts skidding. Interesting, isn't it? Does this mean that cybernetic control systems are capable of "looking ahead?"

That is a topic we will deal with when it comes to management and governance. The question is, after all: "What precisely triggers the control action?" With technical systems, it usually works very well these days.

New Governance by Cybernetics: Communication and Control

The word "cybernetics" comes from the Greek *kybernetes*, which means "helmsman." It is contained in terms such as governor, gouverneur, and governance. As early as 1867, James C. Maxwell wrote a "Theory of Governors." It was an arithmetic generalization of the centrifugal force governor, which James Watt used at industrial scale in his steam engine.

Cybernetics is the science of steering, regulation and control. It becomes particularly interesting and significant when problems arise for which a general, everyday understanding is no longer sufficient. That is the case with all the complex systems I have discussed in the previous chapter. But what precisely needs to be regulated or controlled? In essence, there are three questions to be answered at the top level of an organization:

- WHAT should the institution do?
- WHERE does the institution need to function?
- HOW does the institution need to function?

How the godfather of modern cybernetics, the American mathematician Norbert Wiener, came to occupy himself with cybernetics and who else played a significant role – that would be a story of its own. What matters at this point is the title that Norbert Wiener chose for his 1948 book: *Cybernetics – or Control and Communication in the Animal and the Machine.*

Cybernetics was perhaps the most important science of the 20th century. However, the public debate at the time focused much more on nuclear physics than it did on cybernetics. Still, cybernetics is the science that transforms the 20th into the 21st century.

It is fundamentally changing our lives. Without cybernetics there would be no computers or robots today, no electronics or information sciences, no internet, and no digitalization. Hospitals would have no intensive-care units and no non-invasive surgery; the shipping industry would still navigate with a magnetic compass; airplanes would have to make stopovers due to bad weather conditions; space travel would not exist. In industrial manufacturing and logistics, we would have gotten stuck in the 1960s. There would be neither breakthroughs in biological disciplines nor genetic engineering.

The progress associated with cybernetics – as with any other science – creates risks but even greater opportunities. Cybernetics also provides us with the knowledge required to avoid the risks and take advantage of the opportunities.

The driver is *cybernetics* and the closely related sciences of complexity, *systems theory*, *information the-*

ory, and *communication theory*. They have enabled us to understand and explain the third basic component of reality, *complexity*, as well as – closely related to it – *information and order*, and use them in a systematic manner.

Up to that point, science had only known two basic components of reality: *matter* and *energy*. They are the "subjects" that physics and chemistry focused on in the era of the Enlightenment, attempting to reduce all manifestations of nature to these two components. No doubt this research approach brought an enormous increase in insight and, as a result, in technical possibilities. By integrating the third basic component, we can now understand how complex systems function, and even make them function properly.

Incidentally, the most interesting developments, in my view, are happening not only in technical areas and information sciences but in *life sciences*. There, they mainly originate from the neurosciences – the investigation of brains and central nervous systems. This is not very surprising, seeing that it is the central nervous system which steers, controls, and guides an organism. Brain research without cybernetic findings and concepts would not be imaginable today.

Cybernetics is a science of its own. It is based on the insight that there are *natural regularities* determining the control and regulation, and thus the functioning, of *all* systems. It does not matter at all – and this in itself was a discovery of enormous significance –

whether we are dealing with artificial or biological, physical, technical, social or economic systems.

This is what makes cybernetics a cross-boundary, *transdisciplinary* and universal science, which means much more than "interdisciplinary". And it is what caused Norbert Wiener to give his book the meaningful subtitle "*... in the Animal and the Machine*", thus addressing the closing of the gap between the natural and the artificial word, which had blocked the understanding of complex systems since antiquity.

Cybernetics for Self-Capabilities

"Organize a system so as to make it self-organizing."
Stafford Beer

So far, I have been talking about regulating and steering, of control, and communication. That implies that there must be *somebody* to do this. But cybernetics does not stop there: it takes the eminently important step toward all systems complex enough to have what I call *self-capabilities*. I am talking about self-regulating, self-controlling and self-organizing, self-adjusting, self-repairing, self-curing and self-developing – that is, self-evolving – systems.

One of the key terms of cybernetics is the kind of "systemic control" resulting from the self-capabilities listed above. Prof. Stafford Beer, the founder of management cybernetics, subsumed his works as "The Managerial Cybernetics of Organization."

Cybernetic management, or the other way round – management cybernetics – is the application of advanced cybernetics to complex systems of society, in order to promote holistic management of all kinds of organization. Management cybernetics also means mastering complexity.

Doing Business Is Not Enough

Management, as it is usually understood and taught today, has resulted from a grave yet institutionalized error. Management is considered to be a part of business administration, as it has always been equated with the leading of commercial enterprises. Consequently, it is assigned to the Business Administration faculties, or in the Anglo-American education system to the business schools.

That is not where it belongs, though. The very fact it ended up there explains a major part of the unfortunate developments we have seen in the management of corporations and other organizations.

So, where *does* management belong? What is its purpose? As such, management is not related to doing business, although it can be used for that purpose. Much more, management is related to *functioning*.

It can best be understood as the function of society that enables a society's organizations and systems to function properly. The scientific basis for that is cybernetics: it helps us understand how and why something does or does not function.

So, management would actually belong among the disciplines that deal with functioning, or with regulating, steering, controlling, and shaping. The common generic term for these is control.

Understood correctly, management is applied cybernetics – applied to organizations of any kind. Historically, it did not originate from business, as most people believe. That is just where it has been applied and developed most systematically. It is in businesses where the differences between good and bad management or between right and wrong management are easiest to see, mainly because of all organizations, commercial enterprises are those where bottom-line results are easiest to see and to verify. As a consequence, success and failure can be determined quickly and easily.

And while all other organizations, such as theaters, schools, hospitals, universities, cities, government departments, police, rescue services, and so on do have to generate revenues as well, that is not their purpose. Yet all of them need to function.

Chapter 7

COMPLEXITY FOR THE FUNCTIONING OF ORGANIZATIONS

> "Man in his social and political existence
> must have a functioning society just as he must have air
> to breathe for his biological existence."
> *Peter F. Drucker*

So, what are the solutions for the challenges described – that is, for designing and steering complex organizations so as to enable them to thrive? The answer relates to organizations and to the people working in them.

Two Levels of Functioning

To achieve good solutions, we need to distinguish two different levels within the functioning of organizations. The differences between them are tremendous but they are usually overlooked or confused. It usually helps to approach cybernetic management based on an analogy to the human organism.

In medicine we distinguish between anatomy and physiology. Anatomy includes organs, muscles, and limbs. Physiology includes processes such as blood circulation, breathing, and digestion. This is comparable to how organizations function: their "organs" are corporate functions such as marketing, human resources, finance and accounting, research and development, manufacturing plants, sales organizations, and subsidiaries. These elements are depicted in organization charts. Typical operational processes include doing basic research, engineering, negotiating, selling, delivering, assembling, and procuring. They are depicted in dedicated process charts and form part of the process organization.

In addition to its anatomy and physiology, the human body has a nervous system as well. Its counterpart in organizations is the management system. Note that I am not referring to the persons or groups called "management" but to the *control and regulation processes* that run alongside each operational process and ensure its proper functioning. This element is usually not depicted in organizational diagrams and manuals. In most of them, management is equated with people or bodies of people.

And while a medical doctor would never ignore the nervous system, even hospitals usually forget to depict its counterpart in their organizational diagrams.

Without the nervous system our body could not function; likewise, no organization could function properly without its control and regulation processes – or management. Hence, my understanding that management is the function that enables the systems and organizations of an institution to function properly.

The nervous system is comparable to management processes. That is where the cybernetics of functioning takes place: the control and regulation of operational processes. That is also where communication takes place – via the neural pathways – as communication is what controls the processes. Remember the term "control by communication". That is where we find countless, partly very sophisticated and highly specialized system controls. It is also the source of requisite variety, which, according to Ashby's Law, is needed to cover the organism's variety.

This is visible from the fact that the nervous system extends all the way to the organism's outermost and finest capillaries, interconnecting organs and processes – usually not in the sense that a cable or line does, but by forming its own network, known to experts as "anastomotic reticulum."

The capillary nerves reach the brain in condensed form via the spinal cord, where the controls of organs and processes are assigned to certain, rather stable zones. A particularly richly interconnected and complex brain structure is the cerebellum, the control system in charge of the locomotor system. The latter is one of the most complex components of the organism, and therefore, needs a particularly sophisticated control system. In cybernetics, this is called high-variety system.

In robotics, such high-variety systems present enormous challenges when it comes to controlling motion sequences. The most elegant solution so far has been created by a Swiss scientist specializing in artificial intelligence, Rolf Pfeiffer. He demonstrates impressively how simple the controls even of highly complex systems and processes can be.

Operational and Management Tasks

I subsume corporate bodies and processes under "operational level" or "operational tasks." The nervous system is represented by the – in terms of logic – higher level, the "management level." Every process needs management, although there can always be several solutions for this. Just think of the traffic-light crossing and the roundabout. That is why both are required to ensure proper functioning: processes and process controls. It should be clear by now why these two levels have to be distinguished sharply to avoid confusion.

The first level can vary greatly, depending on the type of organization. Government departments' operational tasks are very different from those of business enterprises, and hospitals' tasks differ from those of opera houses. An automotive company has different things to do than a bank.

By contrast, control tasks at the superordinate management level are always the same, no matter whether it's a government department, a business, or a hospital, an automotive company or a bank. Management is always about the same five key tasks: 1. providing objectives, 2. organizing, 3. making decisions, 4. supervising, and 5. developing people. Further details can be found in my book *Managing Performing Living*.

There I also describe the management tools needed in every organization. There are seven: 1. meetings, 2. reports, 3. job design, 4. personal working methods, 5. budgeting, 6. performance appraisal, and 7. systematic "waste disposal."

This distinction even includes the organizational culture, an area where the general confusion may be greatest. At the level of operational tasks, the cultures even of otherwise very similar organizations tend to be very different. At the management level, however, the prevailing culture must be the same or at least very similar, as you always need a culture of performance, professionalism, and effectiveness – the cultural values of functioning.

Constants in Change: Master Controls

So how do you manage an entire organization or its subsidiaries? How do you manage a hospital and its departments? Or a country's healthcare system? By using master controls – the organization's supreme rules and regulations.

Remember I talked about conditions of utmost complexity, of self-reinforcing dynamics, and irremediable uncertainty. In practice, the question is: *How should I act today, assuming that I cannot know what the future will be like?*

We get to the core of functioning of an organization, irrespective of its type and outer form, when we describe the policy steering the system. Policy means mastering complexity by regulating through laws and rules.

It is the same for any functioning organization, where the policy is determined by its purposes, values, rules, and objectives. These regulators are the result of normative decisions. They are normative when they are original, general, timeless, and without giving detailed reasons.

This is where we have the source of cybernetic self-capabilities. Good corporate policy rules enable a number of employees – an unlimited number in principle – to self-coordinate, to self-organize, and to act purposefully, independently, and adequately in each individual situation. This is how the critical regulating impact in complex circumstances is achieved. In short:

Control = rule x number of its applications + feedback

When rules like these are effectively put in force, top management can sit by, as it were, and watch the system operate on its own – provided you have additionally installed the systems needed to indicate out-of-control incidents.

How Master Controls Work

The navigation and steering of complex systems is achieved with system-cybernetic controls. As the name suggests, they have an unlimited controlling effect on the entire system. They are systemic navigators, and their importance grows along with a system's complexity. It is the same in nature. DNA exercises its control across the whole organism, in every single cell. It is system-wide control. Whatever happens "out there" in the organism and its environment is included in this control through the genetic code. So, what we need in any organization is a counterpart to the genetic code.

In practice, the respective controls for present-day organizations – the navigation instruments – are: purpose, mission, policy, governance, and strategy. In order to ensure these can be effective across the whole system, a certain kind of structure is needed as well – the Viable System structure – and so is a certain culture – the Culture of Effectiveness – as well as executives that master their profession.

Functionally, a part of these controls resembles the genetic code. Master controls are rules that remain constant over time or can only be changed under certain circumstances. The rules governing a possible change are also part of the master controls. They are the constants in change.

A very early, yet still excellent example is the famous Benedictine Rule, written by St. Benedict of

Nursia in 529 A.D. to determine a "DNA" for the order of the Benedictines. It provided the basis for effectively organizing the standardization of medieval monasticism. A facsimile of the Rule – the *Codex Sangallensis 914* – can be found in the Abbey Library of St. Gallen.

System Policy

> "Effective Executives don't make many decisions.
> They solve generic problems through policy."
> *Peter F. Drucker*

Master control by way of system policy is fundamentally different from the traditional perceptions of corporate policy which, in essence, are based exclusively on economics. It is comprehensive systems policy that triggers the evolutionary leap from regulation to self-regulation and from organization to self-organization by making use of system-immanent forces.

Controlling, steering, and regulating are all different expressions for the same thing: managing. They all basically mean the same: creating order where otherwise there would be none, and providing direction where it is missing. Regulating is achieved with rules. System-compatible regulation always follows the same cybernetic logic.

In a cybernetic sense, governance means *managing a system so as to ensure it will be able to self-manage, self-regulate, and self-organize.*

Master controls must be designed according to certain principles with regard to their content and form. After all, it is always possible to write commonplace statements or nonsense in an organizational policy. It regularly happens when the purpose of controls has not been understood – in these cases, the creation of a policy degenerates into mere tokenism.

To avoid that, there are rules for determining both the content and phrasing. The purpose of the controls themselves also plays a key role: *their content represents decisions on the organization's operations and functioning which are indefinite in time*. These decisions are valid until there are external or internal signals indicating a possible change in requirements.

Note that according to the two-level concept, controls as regulatory tools must be distinguished from the operations of the organization. Their formulations can vary, depending on the type of organization, but their effect is always the same. For instance, there are hospital policies and corporate policies; universities have their explicit purpose (usually documented in time-honored statutes) and so do airports.

How significant and powerful these controls can be is quite evident when considering the example of an organization's purpose. It makes quite a difference whether the purpose has been defined as creating shareholder value or satisfying customers – and the organization will have to be managed very differently in each case. At the end of the day, the shareholder value purpose preprograms a corporation's eventual demise, while the purpose of creating satisfied customers will guarantee its continuous prosperity.

Modes of Organization

Modes of organization are another tool helping to manage complex systems. The mode of a system is the way it behaves. With the master control called "mode", you can determine or change a series of basic general states or programs of an organization. In cybernetics jargon, the possibility to control a system by selecting from a range of modes, is referred to as "redundancy of potential command."

Typically – and importantly – the modes must be mutually exclusive. A system can only be in one mode at a time. In the case of organisms, for instance, typical modes include sleeping, eating, fleeing, attacking. An animal cannot flee and eat at the same time, or fight and drink.

In any of these modes, only certain behaviors are possible for optimum performance. In addition to a system's behavior, a change of modes can also cause a change in its organization. As a consequence, you basically have a variety of organizations at your disposal – a phenomenon that can be observed, for instance, when a crew of firefighters switches from standby to emergency mode.

Getting the organization into its situation-specific mode of behavior quickly enough whenever needed is part of the top management task. All of its activities must then be subordinated to one overriding priority. Making this decision is an act of true leadership, in particular due to the enormous impact on the overall organization and in view of the risks involved in wrong decisions. It is also the most effective way to lose leadership, for how many times can you announce a fire alarm by mistake without irrevocably losing your credibility?

For organizations, I have defined the following seven modes. They are basically applicable to all types of organizations:

- Mode 1: Business as Usual,
- Mode 2: Explicit Pursuit of Growth – usually well accepted by management bodies, investors, unions, and the general public. Mode 2, however, is usually more difficult to implement both effectively and visibly, as natural inertia tends to get in the way. Among other things, it depends on how growth is to be accomplished. Growth based on one's own resources requires a different management focus than growth by acquisition. Growth by increasing sales, without gaining market share or increasing productivity, is comparable to the growth of an undetected cancer.
- Mode 3: Change – and it depends on the type of change how it should best be handled. According to the S-Curve diagram (figure 1), there are three different applications for change management: 1. innovations along the "red curve", 2. building and

developing the "green curve", and 3. the transition from "red" to "green." All three involve very different degrees of complexity, which is why they require different methods and tools.

- Mode 4: Special Case – a very effective master control variety, as it involves a great deal of flexibility. In particular in its test mode version, it is a proven means of achieving innovation and change. It is closely connected to issue management, which we will discuss shortly. The art is in deciding, in each particular situation, whether an issue should be addressed inside or outside the usual problem-solving structures, whether it should be regarded as preliminary and reversible for a while, and at what point in time it should be regarded as definite. There are few things offering so many advantages. Organizations with a sophisticated project management in place usually have no problem with this mode.

- Mode 5: Explicit Retreat – usually difficult; depending on whether the retreat will affect only parts or the entire organization. Investors will respond differently compared to employees and unions. Often, a retreat will collide with managers' self-image and the expectations they face inside and outside the organization. Even with a partial retreat, there is often hesitation and passive or even active resistance. Military organizations are a totally different story: retreat is part of the standard repertoire of every commander and the troops are trained accordingly.

- Mode 6: Mastering a Crisis and mode 7: Emergency are activated much too late in most cases. They often hit the company unexpectedly because people lack the courage to face up to the situation in due time. It usually takes too long to get decisions approved by the organizational bodies, which is why their implementation is often difficult. This, however, is precisely where leadership is needed.

A change of modes, if successful, can be enormously effective. You can see that in any organization specifically trained for it, such as emergency organizations, military, or hospitals. In other cases, changes of modes are difficult. They require the new methods pertaining to the Syntegration technology, which I will explain at a later point. For the conditions of the Great Transformation21 and its three challenges – the red curve, the green curve, and the transition zone – the change mode is obviously the right choice. The organization must dedicate its undivided attention and all its strengths to dealing with the challenges of the transformation.

Organizational Issues

Issues are special topics of temporary yet enormous significance, which require basic thinking from an integrated perspective as well as top management authority, and need to be handled outside the usual process rules.

Issue management helps to keep organizations flexible, balancing permanently valid policies with significant special considerations. As outlined before, a system policy defines the organization in its basic features and over the long term. It therefore increases complexity to the extent required for proper functioning; that is, to a point where it enables a relevant number of employees to self-organize. At the same time, the policy also defines rules and thus reduces complexity. Both are necessary.

In developing a policy, you can obviously only use the information you have at the time. But since the organization and its environment will not stand still, top management must permanently check new developments as to their relevance for their current policy. The selection filter is included in the policy itself; it determines the relevance for selecting issues to be dealt with.

Designed to increase flexibility and variety, issue management is the deliberate interruption or circumvention of established organizational and personal approaches and responsibilities, so that a given matter can be addressed strictly according to its *importance* for the greater whole.

Issue management is more than what we usually mean when we refer to top-priority issues. It means dealing with a challenge *outside* established organizational patterns.

Owing to the master control effect of good organizational policy, in particular when based on a sophisticated management system, management capacity is freed up for things that would otherwise take a back seat to everyday operational matters or would be settled on an ad-hoc basis, and which usually get much too little attention and/or are ignored. Ignoring can help – but only with unimportant matters.

Navigation Assistants for the Great Transition

In our search for better solutions, over the years we discovered a good dozen system-cybernetic solutions – methods and tools – that help top executives navigate during the transition phase. They facilitate the control of organizations and provide a clear view on things.

With these navigation assistant tools, top management will find it easier to solve its difficult task, determine its current position, and identify appropriate next steps.

The tools are based on the *real-time control* principle. Specifically, they include the organizational co-ordination "hubs", the operations rooms, the Viable System Model, sensitivity modeling, and Syntegration communication. Lots of new terms, you may think. Yes, that is true – and it is because these are all new tools. Old language is not appropriate for navigating through new times, old maps do not help to discover new territory.

Together, these tools add up to a powerful social technology that helps transform organizations from the "red curve" to the "green curve".

Real-Time Control

It was a fundamental discovery of cybernetics that organisms function according to the real-time principle. At any given point in time, living beings have the information they need at that point about themselves and their environment. Through powerful feedbacks, every change is reported back in real time to the control centers of the nervous system.

The result is a closed circle between sensory and motor functions across the entire system, integrating the organism and its environment into one whole. Every motion change will immediately "appear on the screen." The brain's information on the combined state of the body and environment corresponds to the actual facts at that particular time. Thus, the interaction of more and more precise sensory organs and motor systems and their real-time information links have led to the evolution of more and more advanced forms of life which are able to prevail in more and more complex environments.

We apply this principle very naturally in our daily lives. It would be hard to imagine life without it. Safe driving at night or through foggy weather is hardly imaginable without the real-time controls in driver assistance systems. Today, they are part of the sophisticated navigation systems that have become standard in modern vehicles. They help to make driving safer for ordinary drivers even under most adverse conditions.

It depends on a system's change dynamics what real-time means in the particular case. For instance, a driver will always need to know the car's current speed. For the fuel level and oil pressure, longer intervals are in order, although critical lows are indicated actively, once again reinforcing the real-time principle.

The Hub Principle and One-Person Responsibility

The hub function can best be observed at major airports, where tower controllers are in charge of coordination. The system has a fitting name: "air traffic control."

The hubs – the communication nodes or star points of the network – must be organized in such a way that *in one place* there is full knowledge *at any time* as to whether everything is in control or an intervention is required. To achieve this, the principle of *One-Person Responsibility* must be established: this refers to cybernetic controls that can be derived from organisms and the way their nervous systems and brains function. In air traffic these functional principles are standard. Without them, nothing would function properly. They have to be learnt, though, and supported by sophisticated technology for optimal reliability.

The hub organization combines the advantages of both decentralized and centralized structures. Most organizations take pride in the degree of decentralization they have achieved, and it has often taken them years of intense efforts. Decentralization works the better, the less the system's individual elements – business units, product lines, departments, locations, and subsidiaries – need to be interconnected.

The greater the pace of change, however, the more will decentralization have to be complemented and overlaid with a new centrality of information flows. Its purpose is not to interfere with people's decision spheres or tasks, but to ensure that timely interventions are possible *if and when* something goes wrong.

Organisms and nervous systems are organized the same way. Although the individual organs work independently, pain signals will directly report back to "headquarters" whenever something is wrong. Cancer is an exceptional situation where the system does not work that way. It grows quietly and often will not begin to hurt until it is too late.

Center of Control: The Operations Room

Air traffic controllers have long been familiar with mega-hubs. During military maneuvers, the first thing to do is not to move the troops but to install coordination and command centers. Space flight, too, is managed from integrated control centers, and the same is true for sports events, emergency centers, power plants, and complex manufacturing plants. In the management of organizations, such mega-hubs are still a rarity.

These centers carry different names, such as "combat information center" or "action information center", or simply "operations room." Operations rooms are physical manifestations of real-time control. They are meeting rooms for those high-level experts that manage a complex operation – such as a space mission – from A to Z, 24 hours a day, seven days a week. Once everything has gone well, they will report "mission complete." In the event of an unplanned incident, this is where the change of modes – as discussed above – is initiated for the entire organization. This is where the status information appears on the screens; this is from where action signals are sent to the decentralized operational units.

With a properly functioning operations room, you can manage even the most complex tasks that seemed unmanageable before. And even rather low-tech operations rooms – equipped with flip charts, pin boards, manual updates and so forth – usually lead to a quantum leap in terms of functioning.

The moment you stop using them – as we have done for the sake of experimenting – the system will return to its state of paralysis. Nothing works well, anxiety spreads, and the atmosphere is poisoned by aggression and finger pointing. A system out of control ...

However, the state of paralysis passes just as quickly once the operations room is reactivated, and shortly afterwards work will be enjoyable again, even on very complex projects, because everything is "in control" again.

Nervous Systems for Organizations:
The Viable System Model

How can we make modern matrix organizations function properly? How can we dismantle silos? How can we reduce the amount of red tape in public administration, corporate headquarters, and international organizations? How can we dissolve the logjams and intractable conflicts that in conventional organizations tend to occur and grow like cancerous tumors? These are the key questions addressed by organizational cybernetics.

The *Viable System Model (VSM)* is one of the major discoveries of organizational cybernetics which can help us solve questions like these. We owe it to Stafford Beer, with whom I had a long-standing working relationship and friendship since the mid-1970s. The Viable System Model is the abstract model of the human central nervous system. A model represents what we know about something, including the blank spaces of our non-knowledge – the "white spots" on the map.

The purpose of the Viable System Model is to provide a template for "innervating" an organization. Hence, the VSM is the general-purpose template for using a cybernetic control system, modeled after the central nervous system, in an organization. It integrates all controls discussed so far: the hubs, the operations room, the sensitivity models, and much more.

It was a real surprise for us when we found that it enabled us to *reorganize without moving any boxes.*

"I beg your pardon?" I hear you say. Yes, it is true. The trick is in "rewiring" the different organizational units. What managers rightly hesitate to tackle are major restructuring efforts in which the physical elements, departments, factories, sub-organizations, are changed physically: split up, combined, rebuilt, or eliminated. They do not mind if these elements change how they function, however, as long as this can be achieved in another way.

When the transmission of nerve impulses to the heart does not function properly, we need a pacemaker. It does not matter where it is located. It could basically be at a special-purpose hospital thousands of miles away, sending signals for this particular heart from its data cloud. When the software needs modification, it can be done without heart surgery. New updates of operational systems can be uploaded to our computers without us having to change anything about our programs.

The important thing is that the virtual "wires" to and from our heart are connected properly on both sides, so that the stimulating impulses are provided precisely in the physiologically right way. The heart itself remains where it is. There is no need for "restructuring" or "reorganizing" – things are "refunctioned." The heart receives a new hub.

While this may sound a bit bizarre it is a reality for many tasks – not just medical ones – in aviation and space flight. We separate the reorganization of "anatomical-physiological" elements from "neuro-cybernetic" functioning. This offers enormous organizational improvement potential in terms of flexibility, adaptiveness, acceleration, and performance.

Modeling the Sensitivity of Organizations' Feedback Loops

> "… that the connecting invisible strings behind things are often more important for occurrences in the world than the things themselves."
>
> *Frederic Vester*

Feedback loops are invisible to the eye, just like the capillary nerve fibers in our finger tips. However, from the behavior of a system we can infer that there must be feedback loops in this place, or otherwise the system would function differently. If my finger suddenly gets numb, something must be wrong.

When we know where to look, we can find the causes of things. To ensure we look in the right places, the method of bio-cybernetic sensitivity modeling helps. Its name relates to the ability to detect sensitive organizational concerns and the cause-effect relationships between them. Scientific pioneers in this area were Dietrich Dörner and Frederic Vester.

With sensitivity modeling, we can identify destabilizing feedback loops in organizational behaviors, diagnose cybernetic deficits, and determine ways to eliminate them. Medically speaking, we get something like the modern version of an X-ray of the circuits –

which are often intermeshed in 100 ways – and are able to identify the sensitive switching nodes.

Even by just changing a single algebraic sign from plus to minus, we can change a system radically: from gridlock to release, from paralysis to vitality, from loss to gain.

Social Technologies for Change: Syntegration

How can we integrate the knowledge of an organization, which is distributed over hundreds of individuals, in order to master complex challenges? How can we win over people for the journey into unknown territory? How can we leverage the intelligence and energy tied up in an organization?

The cybernetic communication processes of the Syntegration methodology makes these things possible, and several times more effectively and quickly than with any other approach. Remember the definition of cybernetics: "control by communication."

Syntegration is a high-performance communication approach for managing complexity, interconnectedness, and rapid change. Large numbers of people – as many as are needed – find new solutions for complex questions by communicating simultaneously and in an interconnected manner (resembling the interconnections in a human brain); and in such a way that their joint knowledge, experience, and collective intelligence and their social energy lead to new solutions.

Two laws of nature provide the foundations for this: *By joining what used to be separate, new things are created. And by doing simultaneously what used to be done sequentially, new things are created faster and faster.* The laws of interconnectedness and simultaneity are among the most powerful design resources for a New World.

With syntegrative communication, moods and attitudes can be changed quickly and sustainably, and so can cultural values. The sluggishness of conventional methods is transformed into New World ease. These communication and decision approaches are accelerators and amplifiers for mastering transformation, for changing an organization's mode of operation, and for the quick and effective implementation of results.

I have pointed out the limits to conventional problem-solving methodologies – small teams, mid-sized meetings, large-scale conferences – when discussing the drivers of the Great Transformation21. All three are overstrained by highly complex challenges.

For instance, the challenges of demography, ecology, science, research, and their application require the interaction of numerous experts representing a variety of disciplines. A lot depends on the effectiveness of the exchange and communication among numerous experts from the most diverse areas, each with its own terminology and dealing with its own highly complex issues and relationships.

Chapter 8

HEURISTICS: NAVIGATION PRINCIPLES FOR NEW TERRITORY

"The algorithm is too simple for our world."
Rupert Riedl

I have touched on the subject of algorithms earlier, when discussing our daily life in a digitalized world. Algorithms are as old as mathematics itself. Their big sister, heuristics, goes back even further. It will gain even more importance as we experience and explore the Great Transformation21.

Algorithms are sequences of steps to get to a clearly specified target. Heuristics are sequences of steps to determine the direction and proximity of a target we cannot determine precisely. You know *what* the target is, but you do not know *where* it is.

That may sound a bit abstract, but it gets easier to understand when you consider the example of games: for every game there are rules defining *how to play* it. These are the algorithms. Then there are rules defining *how you win*. These are heuristics.

Mikhail Botvinnik, the great Russian chess world champion, wrote a very noteworthy study on the system rules for winning a game of chess. One of his results was heuristics: *Strengthen your position with every move* – even if you cannot know why and for what. Is that a banality? Perhaps it is. But it is highly effective. It is banal only for those that do not know that the complexity of a game of chess permits 10^{155} moves – that is a one with 155 zeros. Managing an organization, however, is even more complex than a game of chess.

Below is a selection of classic strategic principles for mastering complex situations. Many of them are as old as the hills. They are often mistaken for strategies to acquire and retain power. In fact, they do not have very much to do with power. Their actual nature is to provide direction and orientation in complex circumstances, about which we cannot know enough but in which we have to prove ourselves nevertheless.

Based on these heuristics, one could say that the places of seemingly great power are often places of great powerlessness – and vice versa.

The following principles have not originated directly from cybernetics. As mentioned before, they are much older; yet they are cybernetic in nature because they provide control where other means fail.

Principles for Assessing a Situation in Circumstances of Uncertainty

- *Principle of meta-systemic assessment of the situation*
  "Always make sure to distinguish subject-specific issues from systemic issues." One example: will the best scientist of a university also be the most capable candidate for president? And even if that is the case, will it be good for the university to appoint him president? Questions like these cannot be resolved at the subject-specific level, but only at the system level.

- *Principle of making a complete assessment of the situation*
  "Consider your non-knowledge and search for the entirety of the system." When systems are complex and hypercomplex, you can never have complete knowledge. This principle is a constant reminder of our inevitable not-knowing. More importantly, it reminds us to avoid assessing a situation from our own perspective, as well as thinking in simplified cause-and-effect relationships. What we need to do is reflect on all sides to a relationship, as well as on the relationship itself.

- *Principle of the open system*
  "Always be ready for the unpredictable, the unexpected, and the unimaginable." In complex and dy-

namic systems, unforeseen things can always happen. When continuous change is at work, it can always bring new developments. In an emergency ward, for instance, people are ready for this at any given time. In many organizations they are not.

- *Principle of "strengths against weaknesses"*
  "Never assume others know less than you do." Balances of power must always be viewed realistically. Ignoring this principle is all the more harmful, the more difficult it is to appraise the other side. It indicates the possibilities and limits of sensible behavior – an indispensable feature in both competitive and collaborative situations.

- *Principle of selecting complementary goals*
  "Choose measures that allow you to approach several targets at once." Control interventions working toward several targets at a time will increase, even multiply, effectiveness by utilizing complexity.

- *Principle of avoiding being influenced by slanted information*
  "Make sure you know the sources and key messages of the information you receive." This principle reminds us that in assessing a situation, we should never let ourselves be influenced by carefully collected data without considering the nature and source of those data. At the same time, we should be aware that there are many numerous deception

and obfuscation tactics that form part of the reality of complex systems, both in interpersonal everyday relationships and in competitive ones.

Principles for Control Capacity and the Shaping of Relationships

- *Principle of flexibility*
  "Maintain your room to maneuver and commit yourself at the last possible point." This is about remaining open for future developments, so we will be able to react flexibly to both unforeseeable events and to events that turn out to be unfavorable as things progress.

- *Principle of providing for the future*
  "Verify the type of risk." There are risks we can afford to take, and there are those we cannot afford to take. Then there are risks we cannot afford not to take. All strategic measures have to be checked as to their potential future impact, and we must make sure we have or can obtain the necessary resources for the scenarios that might materialize. The key is to take on risks only to the extent that, even in the case of severe losses, you retain the ability to master any situation.

- *Principle of reversibility*
  "Consider whether you will be able to reverse your decision, and what could follow from such rever-

sal." It is important to get a clear picture of where decisions will be irreversible and where they can be reversed.

- *Principle of sequential go/no go decisions*
  "Do not take the next step until you have seen the impact of your previous step." This principle gains importance as situations get more complex. Based on which intermediate results can we evaluate the impact of an approach? This takes a deliberate point-of-no-return management. Once you have passed the point of no return without noticing, it is too late.

- *Principle of keeping the initiative*
  "Keep ahead of change." I have postulated this before. This heuristic expresses that you need to determine or at least have a say on the sequence of steps to be taken, in order to avoid being put in a tight spot, having to play by rules set by those who got there before you.

- *Principle of monitoring your options*
  "Act always so as to increase the number of options." It was Heinrich von Foerster who formulated this perfect imperative.

- *Principle of the golden bridge*
  "Always maintain an opportunity to talk." One thing to avoid at all costs is forcing your counterpart

into a deadlock. In dealing with other people, this is about avoiding loss of face and maintaining an ultimate basis for discussion, so as to be able to reestablish a control-relevant relationship at some point.

Principles for Information

- *Principle of proximity to information*
  "Keep information paths short and direct." This principle is crucial for avoiding distortions and the unchecked filtering of information. It reveals the significance of a system-compatible organizational policy. Policies that are generally and indefinitely valid fulfill, at any place and any time, the requirements to necessary real-time information; no matter where management bodies are at the time and whether they can or cannot be reached.

- *Principle of explaining one's actions*
  "Say what you do." This principle is targeted at building trust by making incalculable situations predictable by announcing your intentions – for instance, along the lines of, "When such and such happens, I will ..." Of course, this only works if you then stick to what you have declared.

- *Principle of evaluation*
  "Check the control points of your navigation early on, and continually." No matter whether you deal

with a social or a technical system, this principle is about providing the points of reference that will enable you to see at any given time whether the steps carried out will serve the intended purpose and help to achieve the goal pursued. In road traffic, there are median and marginal strips and traffic signs indicating to drivers whether they are on the right track and heading in the right direction at an appropriate speed. Evaluation helps to ascertain whether sensible policies are being formulated in a sensible way, and communicated and implemented effectively.

Principles for Persuasiveness

- *Principle of reliability*
  "Do what you say." Commitments must be met. It is the key condition for keeping one's power of persuasion, future credibility, reputation, and personal authority.

- *Principle of constancy*
  "Stay true to your word." Few things will undermine your personal credibility more quickly and effectively than renouncing your previously announced intentions. This is not about being principled or stubborn. It makes perfect sense, however, to deviate from previous decisions or attitudes that have proven not to be so smart. If you have to do that, make sure you state your reasons.

My book *Strategy for the Management of Complex Systems* lists more heuristic principles. The ones selected here are rather general in nature and interconnectable. They regulate a multitude of behaviors that result from compliance with individual or combined principles. I have selected these general navigation principles with a view to the current situation of disruption. Contrary to random search processes, these heuristics help to reach an unknown target through deliberate exploration.

Chapter 9

FROM DISRUPTION TO NEW DESTINATIONS

"Now I will see
who is stronger: me or me?"
Johann N. Nestroy

The previous chapter addressed the subject of managing an organization's ability to function. Now, we get to the subject of managing people or, to be more precise, management for people's fitness for life.

In our present-day society, management skills have become one of the prerequisites for everyone's ability to find employment. As mentioned earlier, almost everybody today works in an organization. Hardly anyone is prepared for that, though. It is almost as though you would allow someone to drive a car through road traffic without a driver's license.

In organizations, management is important in several respects. Either you are a manager and have to be able to manage others. Or you have a boss and, in order to be able to work well with him or her, you need basic knowledge about how managers think and act. You also need management skills to work with colleagues.

The starting point for right and good management, however, is always yourself. Being able to manage yourself is a key prerequisite for being able to manage others.

In times of change, you have a reason and an opportunity to reorient and improve your performance capabilities. Whatever you need it for, your personal effectiveness and the achievements following from it are your primary asset and your seed capital for working in any organization. It is a resource you can and should transform into results. In times of change, chances are good in particular for those that have worked on their self-improvement. The society of complexity will measure its own success against the extent to which it is able to function reliably.

On Dealing with Limitations

The transition from an Old World to a New World along the dimensions described here will lead to a fundamental shift of boundaries. What boundaries (if any) will remain unchanged, and which of them will disappear entirely, is difficult to predict. That is why *exploring is more important than analyzing; testing is more important than planning; searching is more important than finding; heuristics are more important than algorithms.*

Navigating in times of change also means looking beyond current boundaries and exploring new bearings and coordinates. For instance, in the early 18th century there was nothing more important than determining longitude. As latitudes could be determined correctly but longitudes could not, there were countless shipping disasters due to lack of orientation. All scholars of the time, including Isaac Newton, worked towards a solution for accurately determining the degree of longitude on the high seas – whether in view of the astronomic prize money advertised by the Queen of England, or in hopes of winning fame and glory. All of them failed …

It took another 40 years until John Harrison, a simple Lincolnshire craftsman – a carpenter by trade and clock maker by passion – finally solved the problem, an accomplishment for which he was vigorously attacked. But Harrison had opened a new geographical world to navigators, and thus a new universe of possibilities.

Transformational changes alter the limits of perception. They alter the categories in which we perceive limits and boundaries, the limits to the language we use to describe our perceptions, and the limits to thought and action. Changes like these also expand the limits of required performance, and those of possible performance. The same is always true for personal capabilities and the working style that determines these capabilities.

I have met many successful entrepreneurs and managers who had changed their working approach, and often even their life style, in the course of their lives;

not necessarily because they had to but because they *wanted to*. It was one of their ways to transcend limits and set out for new shores. It was *leadership on their own behalf*.

You get to a limit – and you have to decide whether you will accept it or not. For a long time in our lives, perceived limits are limitations to our working approach and lifestyle, but they are far from being the actual limits to our performance capabilities.

Leadership on Your Own Behalf

These days, complaints about stress and anything related to it abound. There are so many different resources offered for help that trying out all the tips and advice provided daily is almost too much.

I take the subject of stress seriously, as among thousands of managers that have attended our seminars only very few stated that stress was not an issue. This diverse and comprehensive experience has provided the basis for my own position, which differs substantially from mainstream thinking. Precisely because I take stress, burn-out, and work-life balance seriously, I look for solutions – but I do so in very different directions.

For many years now, my solution has been one that I have not heard or read about anywhere else. This is my advice: *Learn to work so effectively and well that you will not be under stress. Become so effective and professional that you will have a life.* When people first hear this, they usually look at me with big eyes because they have expected something different. Then they begin to think about my words …

In many years of working with managers and in management education, I have often paid particular attention to those of them – often very successful people – who did not seem to feel stressed out. I was interested in seeing whether they had any features in common. Was there anything these women and men shared, a pattern of any kind, a reason why they did not feel stress and why work-life balance was not an issue for them?

The answer is yes. It is always the same five things I observe: 1. These people have a task that provides meaning for their existence. 2. They enjoy sound personal relationships, no matter what their nature, and they discontinue problematic relationships before it is too late. 3. Almost all of them dedicate some of their free time to a good cause and to society. They are not only executives in an organization, but also citizens in an open society. 4. They pursue personal interests beyond their profession, such as the arts, music, literature, or history; they are curious about the world and its beauties. When their profession starts boring them, they have other sources of strength. 5. They live a healthy lifestyle and keep physically fit, as they know how important this is for their spirits and souls.

Continuously Improving Your Personal Effectiveness

Executives' personal effectiveness gains even greater importance in times of change. Many have problems with it, others find it easy to achieve. Where do the differences lie?

In almost all cases, it is two things: people's personal effectiveness and their inner attitude. In addressing the two, I will select the key issues I am regularly confronted with when working with executives.

The key to successful management, and even to a successful life and to navigating through the Great Transformation21 is every individual's personal effectiveness. *Doing the right thing, and doing it the right way* – that is how effectiveness is defined.

Effectiveness is the essence of an executive's profession. It may not be the *reason* for his or her success, but it most definitely is its *foundation*. The task to be performed by managers is *turning resources into results*. These resources include their own talents and strengths, their knowledge and experience. Managing means ensuring that everything functions properly, beginning with yourself.

In times of change, we have to be even more effective because we enter new territory and have to manage the unknown; because former success formulas no longer work; because many of the experiences gathered are no longer useful.

Being more effective does not mean working more. It means working in a *smarter* way. Not more of the same, but new and different. When you work on your self-improvement, you can keep improving all your life. It is my experience that irrespective of your age, you can increase your effectiveness by 5 to 10 percent every year, if you work on it rigorously. So, at 40 years of age you have an almost certain chance to double your effectiveness. Precisely what you do with this growth potential is up to you.

I recommend considering increases in effectiveness not to be a must but a may and a want – an object of the curious behavior that is innate in humans but often neglected. That is how you determine new settings of navigation for yourself. If you were facing a must you would risk getting stuck in old categories, struggling against yourself in a fight you cannot win.

Wherever the transformation eventually turns, you will have a performance reserve. Navigating in times of change also means searching new benchmarks for a new performance capability.

Three points are always critical to your own effectiveness, and they are cumulative: your own time management, the use of your personal strengths, and a strict focus on a few priorities.

About every six months or so, you should keep a diary for about a week for the sake of diagnostics, in order to see what you work on, what you spend your time on, and what you achieve in that time. You will quickly see what you can improve. You will also regularly be surprised at how much time you waste on marginal things.

A particularly helpful principle here is *Stop doing the wrong things*. It enormously facilitates your progress, as it does not postulate the Old World behavior of doing more and more; rather it is a New World principle of discontinuing useless and outdated things – thus, making room for the new.

When Something Is New: Managing by Instructions

Another method that is helpful in coping with change and complexity is managing with directly task-related *instructions*. This is often confused with authoritative behavior, as it looks similar from the outside. In reality it is something completely different from giving orders. It is flexible management through information and communication – by means of tips.

If the current situation is *familiar* to a person, conventional management is in order. In that case, you can leave the What and the How to the employee. If the situation is new, however, and if it keeps changing rapidly, you cannot expect an employee to automatically do the right thing. So you need to actively provide him or her with instructions.

The difference and the useful effect of this method are easiest to see when considering the navigation systems in cars or smartphones. We can use them to guide us, visually and acoustically, to an unknown destination in a city we do not know. "Keep straight for 900 feet, then take a left at the intersection; take the second right turn and after 300 feet turn right into the driveway…"

Instructions like these are not commands in the usual sense, although they are phrased that way. They are *pieces of information whose abidance is recommended for effectively accomplishing a task.* Cooking recipes and rules of etiquette belong in the same category.

In this example, I am talking about the specific help given to a specific person for a specific task. Signage systems at airports fulfil a similar function, in that they are designed as orientation aids for millions of flight passengers who are not known personally nor are their destinations. Each passenger selects what he or she needs at the given time to find his or her destination. If you are at the Zurich airport going to Frankfurt, you pick your terminal, your gate, and your flight number. If you enter your flight data in your smartphone, you will be guided to the right place by continuous real-time updates, no matter where you start.

Systems like these enable people to do the right thing amidst the uncertainty of the new. Instructions and signals provide orientation for our behavior in unfamiliar circumstances, they prevent stress and provide the certainty that we can find our way even in unknown surroundings.

Not Only Communication but also Meta-Communication

Systems, just like individuals and teams, are controlled by information and communication. In complex situations, however, information as such is not enough. It must be a kind of information that lets people know *collectively* that everyone is informed.

That is communication about communication, a higher-level communication if you will. In cybernetics it is called meta-communication. It enables individuals and teams to self-control and, if necessary, self-organize – not only as individuals but especially as a team.

Everyone must know that everyone knows that everyone knows everything required to complete the task. This thought may be unfamiliar to many. Is it not enough if everyone knows what he or she needs to know? Sometimes it is, but more and more often it is not. This is the point where we get to actual cybernetics as the science of communication and control. Bilateral communication alone is not enough to master complex situations. On the contrary, it maximizes the risk of misunderstandings. So, there must be meta-communication simultaneously with bilateral communication.

Managing Your Boss and Colleagues

Your boss and colleagues are at least as important for your success as your own employees, as they, too, belong to "your system" – and in a sense they have to be managed, too. Or, to be more precise, you have to be able to work with them effectively. To achieve that, you need to do something and take the initiative instead of waiting to be invited.

In studies and media reports on stress, on low motivation, and in general on the sufferings in organizations, incompetent bosses, and scheming colleagues are frequently mentioned. However, as you cannot change your boss and colleagues, you have every reason to manage them properly, so you will not have to "endure" them but become effective nevertheless. Following a few simple rules will help.

- *Rule No. 1: Manage your boss and colleagues.*
  90 percent of all people are unaware of this rule, which is why it does not even dawn on them that there could be something they could do. Instead, they get annoyed with their bosses and colleagues, some even to the point of getting ill.

- *Rule No. 2: Find out what kind of persons your boss and colleagues are.*
  What bosses and colleagues are like in general is something you cannot know, and neither do you really have to know it. But over time you can get

to know the few people around you well enough to know what makes them tick. If someone likes reading, send her e-mails. If someone is a listener, better call him. If your boss wants everything on one page, give her one page. If she prefers long essays, give her those.

- *Rule No. 3: Use your boss's strengths.*
  Where bosses and colleagues have their weaknesses is something you usually know soon enough. But where are their strengths? In areas where they have their capabilities, you can help them be even better and more successful. That is what most people want. If you help them by working towards their goals, you will make your career alongside theirs.

- *Rule No. 4: Assume responsibility for mutual understanding.*
  Bosses and colleagues are experts, just like you. Experts often live in the closed-up world of their particular jargon. They usually do not think of expressing themselves differently, and more comprehensibly. That is why you should do that – as an invitation and a bridge the other person can cross.

- *Rule No. 5: Communicate in closed loops.*
  If the situation is truly complex, you need cybernetic feedback to ensure your communication functions reliably. These feedbacks are called order confirmation or implementation reports. One good

example is radio traffic between airplane pilots and their traffic controllers at the tower. The same is true for rule No. 4.

The process is simple and straightforward: every incoming instruction is confirmed. Then you act upon the instruction and report on its completion, which is confirmed by your counterpart. Simple measures such as these can help to make a system function almost 100 percent reliably. Error rates and misunderstandings will dramatically decrease within a very short time, and the system's effectiveness will multiply.

Management as a Passion

The brilliant sociologist Peter Gross, a friend of mine, once said that management was *the passion for the possible*. I find this very much to the point, which is why I chose it as a heading for the final thoughts presented in this book.

It fits particularly well with times of disruption and new destinations. Disruptions open up new opportunities by replacing the old and generating the new. And management, as I see it, is the function of society that permits us to do this effectively, to grasp these opportunities and turn them into realities.

The better you get at your job, the more you usually enjoy it. That may not be the case every single day, but often enough to draw strength and the confidence that in the future you will be able to cope with increasingly greater tasks more and more effectively.

You will acquire mastery in the completion of your tasks and have things in control. You become more effective. Even when you have a lot of work, it will not bring the kind of stress to negatively impact your life.

So, once again: *make it your goal to get so good at your job as a manager in the New World that you will not be under stress. Get so effective and professional that you can take on more and increasingly higher-level tasks and, for that very reason, have time to lead a good life.*

Enjoyment of your job is one way to accomplish what is probably the most important thing in life, far more important than motivation and money: finding your own meaning, as recommended by Viktor Frank, the founder of the concept of meaning in life.

For managers, we can add another dimension of meaning: finding meaning in one's actions by creating opportunities for *others* to find *their* meaning in life through their tasks for and in our society's organizations.

EPILOG

> "... this is a time to make the future –
> precisely because everything is in flux.
> This is a time for action."
> *Peter F. Drucker*

The people I mentioned at the beginning who will readily explain to you what is *not* possible – the nay-sayers – will increase in numbers, as more and more things are actually *no longer* possible, and some *not yet*. This can lead to unbridgeable conflicts, which is why the Great Transformation21 will need more and better leadership than any other transformation in history. Leadership in the phase of change will be crucial to how the New World will look and how well it will function.

It takes more than business administration and economics to make leadership effective in a complex world. It takes a new, right, and good – that is, professional and system-cybernetic – kind of management. It considers management to be the societal function that enables a society's organizations and systems to function reliably and in line with their legitimate purpose, even in conditions of great complexity, and to see more in people than mere economic objects. That is what navigation in the Great Transformation has to aim for. Right and good management also includes socially responsible leadership and governance.

To ensure proper functioning, it takes many leaders at many organizational levels. Leadership theories that still focus on the single hero figure are a thing of the (very) Old World. Such hero figures are politically dangerous when they promote radical and populist ideas. Proponents of such leadership theories are irresponsible; they should and *must* know better.

There are four points – and a fifth that is critical for the New World – that determine whether a person will be considered a leader in his or her organization, and thus have the impact we perceive as leadership. Increasingly, however, in a society of complexity it will not be individuals and their "heroic" deeds that count, but the ability of teams of people to interlink the crucial knowledge in multiple ways to create and implement better solutions. Individuals will continue to have the critical task of identifying the right teams in time for the right challenges. Above all, however, these individuals will have to provide the teams with the right tools for utilizing complexity.

The first sign of true leadership is the ability to set the *right policy*, for wrong policies lead to misleadership, in particular if paired with the charisma constantly demanded by the directionless.

The second sign of leadership is the ability to prepare the organization early enough for the different modes of operation and activate the *right mode* in good time. This requires a clear perspective, realistic assessment of the situation, and personal courage.

The third sign of leadership is the ability to select the *right issues* and make sure they are tackled in the right way. That is topic-related leadership.

The fourth sign of leadership is rules or principles which guide people's actions, and thus the implementation of policies.

A fifth sign of leadership will be crucial for navigating through times of change: navigating and leading with open results.

This may be easiest to understand when using music as an example. Classical symphonies are composed "end to end"; the score is unalterable, specifying every single note and pause. There may be difficult parts but there are no surprises. A classical symphony is not complex, but it can be complicated.

The New World and the transition to it are complex but not "composed end to end." There is no score. They are like symphonies for which the score is created while playing.

One paradigm is jazz music where it was very early to anticipate the new and its complexity. It is open-ended, as is modern art. It improvises, but not in an unstructured way or even at random, although to many people it appears to be, and in free jazz it sounds like it is if you do not recognize the structures and patterns.

Another paradigm is evolution. Its process rules are based on laws of nature, but its outcomes *evolve*.

Its rules include probabilities and propensities. Their purpose is to take advantage of unpredictable changes in complex DNA to ensure a continuously improved functioning in an unpredictable and complex environment.

It is similar with leadership in the Great Transformation21. Its rules are provided in the form of policies and heuristics. Its outcomes evolve in the process. Instead of showing a landscape, its map shows the rules for the emergence of landscapes, and the rules for the emergence of rules for landscapes.

Leaders in the times of profound change will (continue to) be those who understand this, establish new management systems for right navigation across their organizations, and visibly assume the responsibility for both through their actions. We are not at the end, but in the very early phases of complexification of the world, and thus are facing the solution of problems that cannot be solved in the old ways.

Great advances in navigating and steering are possible now that complexity-compatible methods and tools have been invented. They have multiplied our ability to master change, as we no longer have to wait for people to change.

Asking people to change before change is even possible is an approach from the last century. Today, we can give people new methods to cope with change right here and right now.

With every step into the unknown, we learn more about the next steps and about increasingly effective ways to deal with uncertainty. That is what complexity-compatible methods and models with their feedbacks have been designed for. In short, we create the path as we walk it – and shape what emerges, when it emerges.

SOURCES

Ashby, W. R., *An Introduction to Cybernetics*, London 1956.

Bateson, Gregory, *Mind and Nature: A Necessary Unity (Advances in Systems Theory, Complexity, and the Human Sciences)*, Hampton 1979.

– *Steps to an Ecology of Mind*, New York 1972.

Beer, Stafford, *Beyond Dispute, The Invention of Team Syntegrity*, Chichester 1994.

– *Brain of the Firm. The Managerial Cybernetics of Organization*, Chichester, 1972, 1994.

– *Cybernetics and Management*, London 1959.

– *Platform for Change*, London 1975.

Bresch, Carsten, *Zwischenstufe Leben – Evolution ohne Ziel?* Munich, 1977.

Dörner, Dietrich, *Logik des Misslingens. Strategisches Denken in komplexen Situationen*, Reinbek bei Hamburg 1989, updated edition: 2004.

Drucker, Peter F., *Management*, London 1973.

– *Post-Capitalist Society*, New York 1993.

– *The Future of Industrial Man*, New York 1942.

– "We need Middle-Economics", in: Krieg, Walter/Galler, Klaus/ Stadelmann, Peter (Hrsg.), *Richtiges und gutes Management: vom System zur Praxis*, Festschrift für Fredmund Malik, Bern/Stuttgart/Wien 2004.

Foerster, Heinz von, *KybernEthik*, Berlin 1993.

Frankl, Viktor, *Man's Search for Meaning*, Washington 1984.

Gross, Peter, *Die Multioptionsgesellschaft*, Frankfurt am Main 1994, 10.

Hayek, Friedrich A. von, "Die verhängnisvolle Anmassung. Die Irrtümer des Sozialismus", in: Bosch, Alfred/Streit Manfred E./Vanberg, Viktor/Veit, Reinhold (Hrsg.), *Friedrich A. von Hayek. Gesammelte Schriften in deutscher Sprache*, Band 7, Tübingen 1988, 2011.

– *Law, Legislation and Liberty*, 3 volumes, 1973, 1976.

Heinsohn, Gunnar, *Söhne und Weltmacht*, Zürich 2006.

Heinsohn, Gunnar/Steiger, Otto, *Eigentumsökonomik*, Marburg 2006.

Krieg, Walter, *Kybernetische Grundlagen der Unternehmungsorganisation*, Bern 1971.

Marchetti, Cesare, "Fifty-Year Pulsations in Human Affairs", in: *Futures* 17(3): 376 – 388.

– *Intelligence at Work, Life Cycles for Painters, Writers and Criminals, Conference on the Evolutionary Biology of Intelligence*.

Maucher, Helmut/Malik, Fredmund/Farschtschian, Farsam: *Maucher und Malik über Management. Maximen unternehmerischen Handelns*. Frankfurt/New York 2012.

Popper, Karl R., *Die offene Gesellschaft und ihre Feinde*, 2 Bände, Bern 1958.

– *Eine Welt der Propensitäten*, Tübingen 1995.

Polanyi, Karl, [*The Origins of Our Time*] *The Great Transformation*, New York 1944.

Prechter, Robert, Jr., *Pioneering Studies in Socionomics*, 2003.

– *The Wave Principle of Human Social Behavior and the New Science of Socionomics*, 1999.

Riedl, Rupert, *Die Ordnung des Lebendigen, Systembedingungen der Evolution*, Hamburg/Berlin 1975.

– *Strukturen der Komplexität. Eine Morphologie des Erkennens und Erklärens*, Berlin/Heidelberg 2000.

Schumpeter, Joseph, *Capitalism, Socialism and Democracy*, London 1950.

Ulrich, Hans/Krieg, Walter, "Das St. Galler Management-Modell", 1972; wiederveröffentlicht in: Ulrich, Hans, *Gesammelte Schriften*, Vol. 2, Bern/Stuttgart/Vienna 2001.

Vester, Frederic, *Die Kunst vernetzt zu denken*, München 2007.

– *Neuland des Denkens*, Stuttgart 1980.

– *Sensitivitätsmodell*, Frankfurt 1980.

Wiener, Norbert, *Cybernetics, or Control and Communication in the Animal and the Machine*, Cambridge 1948.

SELECTED READINGS BY FREDMUND MALIK

Managing Performing Living: Effective Management for a New World. Campus Verlag, 2006, 2015.

Maucher und Malik on Management: Maxims of Corporate Management. Campus Verlag, 2013.

Strategy for Managing Complex Systems: A Contribution to Managerial Cybernetics for Evolutionary Systems. Campus Verlag, 2016. Based on the 10th edition (2008) of the German original.

Uncluttered Management Thinking: 46 Concepts for Masterful Management. Campus Verlag, 2011.

Bionics – Fascination of Nature. Malik Management Center St. Gallen, MCB-Publishing House, 2007.

Series: "Management: Mastering Complexity":

Volume 1: *Management: The Essence of the Craft.* Campus Verlag, 2010.

Volume 2: *Corporate Policy and Governance: How Organizations Self-Organize.* Campus Verlag, 2011.

Volume 3: *Strategy: Navigating the Complexity of the New World.* Campus Verlag, 2013.

The Right Corporate Governance: Effective Top Management for Mastering Complexity. Campus Verlag, 2012.

INDEX